MEMOIR OF A THINKING RADISH

An Autobiography

PETER MEDAWAR

Oxford   New York

OXFORD UNIVERSITY PRESS

1988

Oxford University Press, Walton Street, Oxford OX2 6DP

Oxford New York Toronto
Delhi Bombay Calcutta Madras Karachi
Petaling Jaya Singapore Hong Kong Tokyo
Nairobi Dar es Salaam Cape Town
Melbourne Auckland

and associated companies in
Beirut Berlin Ibadan Nicosia

Oxford is a trade mark of Oxford University Press

British Library Cataloguing in Publication Data
Medawar, P.B.
Memoir of a thinking radish: an
autobiography.
1. Medawar, P.B.   2. Immunologists—
Great Britain—Biography
I. Title
509'.2'4   QR180.72.M43
ISBN 0–19–282083–4

Library of Congress Cataloging in Publication Data
Medawar, P. B. (Peter Brian), 1915–
Memoir of a thinking radish.
Includes index.
1. Medawar, P. B. (Peter Brian), 1915–
2. Immunologists—Great Britain—Biography. I. Title.
QR180.72.M43A3   1988   616.07'9'0924 [B]   87–22138
ISBN 0–19–282083–4 (pbk.)

Set by Hope Services, Abingdon, Oxon
Printed in Great Britain by
The Guernsey Press Co. Ltd.
Guernsey, Channel Islands

To
two *s*, two *d*

ACKNOWLEDGEMENTS

My secretary and literary assistant Mrs Joy Heys gave me, as always, invaluable help in preparing this book for press. The help of my wife and fellow-author Jean has been most profound.

CONTENTS

LIST OF PLATES

The lives of scientists, considered as Lives, almost always make dull reading . . . It could hardly be otherwise. Academics can only seldom lead lives that are spacious or exciting in a worldly sense. They need laboratories or libraries and the company of other academics. Their work is in no way made deeper or more cogent by privation, distress or worldly buffetings. Their private lives may be unhappy, strangely mixed up or comic, but not in ways that tell us anything special about the nature or direction of their work. Academics lie outside the devastation area of the literary convention according to which the lives of artists and men of letters are intrinsically interesting, a source of cultural insight in themselves. If a scientist were to cut his ear off, no one would take it as evidence of a heightened sensibility; if a historian were to fail (as Ruskin did) to consummate his marriage, we should not suppose that our understanding of historical scholarship had somehow been enriched . . .

Peter Medawar, *Pluto's Republic* (Oxford, 1982), 263

a scientific autobiography belongs to a most awkward literary genre. If the difficulties facing a man trying to record his life are great—and few have overcome them successfully—they are compounded in the case of scientists, of whom many lead monotonous and uneventful lives and who, besides, often do not know how to write . . .

Erwin Chargaff, *Science*, clix (1968), 1448

A scientist's biographer deals with much duller material than does a chronicler of Kings . . . I have found most biographies of scientists remarkably uninteresting and their autobiographies even more so . . .

Salvador Luria

INTRODUCTION

The title needs explaining. For reasons made clear by the book's epigraphs, I was not anxious that it should appear explicitly as the writing of a scientist; it was indeed a special wish not to claim for myself as author any distinction more extravagant than membership of the human race. I thought, then, to devise a title out of one or other of the best-known literary similitudes of man. The first was Pascal's *roseau pensant*—his thinking reed—and the second Falstaff's forked radish (*Henry IV* Part II, iii. 2). Better still, I thought, would be a title that somehow combined the two. I put my problem to the representative of the Harvard University Press in England and her husband, the Provost of King's College Cambridge. 'Why not a thinking radish?' said the Provost, with the grasp of essentials expected of a distinguished philosopher—and so it became.

With most of my writings I have had at the very back of my mind a model of the *kind* of book I should like to write: with *Aristotle to Zoos* (which my wife and I wrote together) it was Voltaire's *Dictionnaire philosophique* and with *Advice to a Young Scientist* it was Lord Chesterfield's Letters to his son; with this autobiographic memoir it has been S. T. Coleridge's *Biographia Literaria* ('Or, Biographical Sketches / of my / Literary Life and Opinions'; London, 1817), a work I enjoyed as much as I should like my own readers to enjoy this.

The pure narrative I have reduced to the very minimum, confining myself to those aspects of my life which seem to me to throw some light on the human comedy or the human predicament—very often the same thing. This, then, is a book of opinions which my life can be regarded as a pretext for holding.

There is no message, therefore, but some themes do recur: one of them is the generally destructive effect upon English social life and our position in the world caused by the infirmity of manners I call 'snobismus'—a syndrome that more aptly than any other deserves to be called the 'English disease'.

Snobismus is the irresistibly exigent impulsion to appear before the world as someone grander and more important in point of family, schooling, wealth, friends, and worldly distinction than one really is—and with this syndrome goes a somewhat debilitating conception of the manners and address that are or are not compatible with gentility. To snobismus, it will be shown in due course, may be attributed some part of the decay of the English theatre, whose renaissance was motivated by the belief that plays should be *about* something —and preferably something that matters. The maleficent effects of this disease of manners are a subject upon which I regard myself as especially well qualified to express an opinion, being ethnically speaking only half English. Now read on.

VERY EARLY YEARS

'You are of Arabic extraction, aren't you?' said the British Ambassador to Lebanon, with characteristic infelicity, introducing me to the principals of the Royal Ballet performing prettily but, because of the height, rather breathlessly in Baalbek. 'I can't bear that expression,' said my closest friend in the Lebanon, Émile Bustani, 'it makes you sound like some kind of gum.'

Like many Phoenicians before him, my father left Jounieh, his birthplace in the Lebanon, and travelled west in search of his fortune, staying briefly in London as a paying guest with my mother's family, the Dowlings, where he fell in love with and in due course married the elder daughter of the family, Muriel, who reappears in these pages later on as Granny Moo. My father took the first steps towards earning a living by becoming the agent in Rio de Janeiro of a British firm manufacturing dental supplies. (I remember an office in the Avenida Rio Branca full of dental chairs and trays of false teeth.) The most comic moments in my youth and early manhood were when schoolfellows or fellow students at Oxford asked me what my father did and I was able to tell them 'He sells false teeth in South America.' It was a joy to see the agonies of embarrassment into which this threw my interlocutors as they struggled to find words to put me at my ease and good-naturedly did their best to relieve me of the burden of shame which they took for granted must weigh upon my every waking moment.

I was born on 28 February 1915 in a suburb of Rio known, felicitously enough, as Petropolis and my birth was registered at the British Consulate in good time to acquire the status of 'natural-born British subject'.

One remembers one's childhood not as a continuous narrative—the first reel of the Medawar story—but rather as a number of tatty film clips such as lie about on the cutting-the days when recordings omitted high treble and bass registers almost completely and were reproduced on gramophones through little tin trumpets such as the dog listens to in the famous HMV trade mark (though I don't remember them giving any less pleasure than is to be obtained from a modern multi-channel recorder in which sound enters through all bodily apertures, however ill-fitted to the purpose, in addition to the two that our Lord wisely set aside with this in mind).

In spite of its many virtues, the gramophone, it must be said, has one aesthetic disadvantage that we come to recognize and guard ourselves against in the course of life. It is the prevalence of the phenomenon of musical imprinting—something akin to that which befell Professor Konrad Lorenz's ducks. In the gramophone world, imprinting takes the form of tending to regard as definitive—as the last word, indeed—the interpretation of a work that we hear first and probably most often, so that any subsequently heard departure from it strikes us as wrong-headed and schismatic.

(But imprinting is all right, of course, if that which is imprinted is superlative of its kind—the recordings by the Busch Quartet, for example, of the last quartets of Beethoven or by Artur Schnabel of his piano sonatas. For me there are no others.)

I learnt in my first term at Magdalen College Oxford that although the gramophone, as a 'mechanical contraption', was an instrument of a kind Mr C. S. Lewis was constitutionally opposed to, he had made it an exception which did not qualify as an engine of the worldwide conspiracy of science and technology against human values—even including my own gramophone, which had a horn seven feet long. He and a favourite pupil, Richard Peile, would often drop into my rooms of an evening to chat and listen to the seabirds that flutter through the symphonies of Sibelius, which were just becoming known in England through the good offices of the Sibelius Society. We both thought these seabirds especially felicitous, though on much else we differed. I once declaimed a little of Nietzsche's poetry to him. 'That's all rot, isn't it?'

said Lewis in the dismissive mood in which he is best remembered. It is not. Many years later, Sir Ernst Gombrich, whose opinions on such matters I have long regarded as law-giving, told me, 'Some of Nietzsche's poetry is really rather good.'

I no longer get anything like the fun out of gramophone records that I had as a boy. This is not because my taste is now for live performances but because for some time past I have been able to buy any record I wanted and this takes all the excitement out of it. I look back nostalgically to the days when I saved my pocket-money for a matter of weeks to buy one gramophone record and I could listen critically on the same occasion to four or five other records in a little private cubicle. Thus buying one record made it possible to entertain oneself with a short musical festival. Buying a record is something I now do through a trusty dealer on the telephone, but it used to be something of an adventure. The records from which I get most pleasure today are reissues on long-playing records of those I liked best in my youth—of operatic pieces sung by Giovanni Martinelli, Ezio Pinza, and Rosa Ponselle—or even all three in concert.

Not the least of the benefactions of the gramophone has been the introduction of a diverting indoor pastime: conducting in front of a mirror, where innumerable superlative perform-ances have taken place. Here the conductor maintains a firm beat with the right hand while using the left hand to bring forward his woodwind in the interests of balance, or shushes his trombones when they threaten to become obstreperous.

The Life of the Mind

A clip from the first reel of my life shows me in a Portuguese infants' school run by a lady called Madame Carvalho (as who, in Brazil, is not?) who enveloped her little pupils in a bosomy embrace as she walked downstairs into the classroom: I cannot remember what she taught but only how strongly she smelled of breakfast. I do however remember with gratitude and admiration the disagreeable and apparently embittered lady in black whose duty it was to teach us the rudiments of arithmetic. I say 'gratitude' because this lady considered it to be her business to teach us addition, subtraction, and the like and so she jolly well did. Teaching was of course all in Portuguese, in which I became reasonably proficient, though nothing now remains except a knowledge of Portuguese pronunciation—especially that ugly nasal *aõ* that is akin to the French *on* in, for example, *bon* or *cochon*, though more strongly nasal.

Children's Comics

My elder brother Philip and I amused ourselves with unremarkable childish pastimes and a highlight of the week was the arrival from England of *The Rainbow*, a more than usually soppy children's magazine produced by that form of colour printing in which the splodges of colour were often not even approximately on target. Children's comics are sociological treasure houses. I remember for example that one such magazine—*Comic Cuts*, I think it was—had a regular weekly strip of which the protagonists, named Nappy and Tallyman, were drawn in such a way as to make it clear that they were Napoleon and Talleyrand, at one time feared and hated people. *The Rainbow*, however, my first reading, had nothing so exciting: the adventures of Tiger Tim, Bobby Bruin, Susie Sunshine, Joey the Parrot, and Georgie Giraffe were rooted on all occasions in a dull propriety. One strip, I do remember, aroused my critical faculties for the first time. It was called 'Susie Sunshine and her Poms'. This idiot trio got into all kinds of scrapes and difficulties, from which they were saved by the intervention *ex machina* of Marzipan the Magician, a touch from whose magic wand instantly mended a broken toy, retrieved the lost sixpence, or conjured up the bounteous meal Susie was in need of. It was so easy that it robbed the story line of all suspense, and I felt about Marzipan what in later life I came to feel about the writings of psychoanalysts and psychohistorians about the origins of psychoses and the springs of human behaviour. And when they got going, the priests of sociobiology were just as mad as Marzipan.

Children's comics went through several stages during my life until the time came for me to pluck from my own children's hands the issue of *Beano* they were hoping to read themselves. How lucky they were, I thought, to have such lively and genuinely comic stuff to read instead of that droopy *Rainbow*.

The best era, I believe, was that in which the comics were peopled by the giants of the contemporary cinema—aristocrats of the screen such as Chester Conklin, Wallace Beery, Harry Langdon, and Buster Keaton. In these all was plain sailing: thieves were identified by having big bags over their shoulders labelled 'SWAG'. Editorial policy was contemptuous of aristocrats and unfeeling towards victims of gout, assumed to be an occupational disease of the high-born, who addressed each other with usages that died with King George III. 'What, what?' and 'Haw, haw' identified the toffs with taxonomic precision and of all the *dramatis personae* the victims of gout were the least Christ-like in point of sweetness of temper and endurance of suffering.

My brother's and my favourite occupation in early childhood was not to read comics, however, but to bathe on Copacabana beach, upon which the town's sewers emptied directly. Around each effluent all the sewage collected in huge stagnant pools, around which the children played. Poliomyelitis, not unexpectedly, was endemic and I don't know why I didn't get it. I suppose it could have been because of repeated exposure to sub-clinical infection.

My Brother Philip

My brother Philip was not so lucky. He was an irresistibly high-spirited and mischievous boy who had already nearly killed himself by playfully shoving a spade between the spokes of the front wheel of a still moving car, as a result of which he broke a leg and was thrown on to his back with such violence that he was irretrievably blinded in one eye by a

property ourselves. Philip, already showing some of the signs of an explosion of maniacal laughter, sat impatiently fidgeting while one officer or another entered or left the room with an air of hushed self-importance. With fatal lack of judgement I leaned over to Philip and said 'All the fuss is because nobody in Lebanon has ever given anything away before.' This was our undoing, for Philip started laughing hysterically and in spite of burning himself repeatedly with a cigarette he was simply unable to bring it under control.

Various legal officers looked at me despairingly until with cowardly disloyalty to my brother I turned towards them and wearing a wise, kind smile tapped my temple in the way traditionally used to signify that someone is not quite right in the head. Fortunately this circumstance was not thought by the Embassy to diminish the validity of the affidavit he had just sworn declaring that he had no interest in our late father's house. We all left in disgrace and Philip started up again outside when I told him we would all continue to be very, very kind to him.

Philip was a good-looking man and in spite of his physical and, as I thought, mental infirmity he was very attractive to women and married two (successively, of course). Because, I suppose, of the frustration he suffered, he ate enormously and became rather obese. 'Peter,' he once said to me, 'why do you think I get a sort of fluttery feeling in my stomach?' Being now a bit fed up with his over-eating, I replied, 'You must try to think of it as a poor caged bird struggling desperately to get out before it is stunned again by the delivery of another huge meal.' I was in no position to advise him, but should not have been so dismissive, for he eventually died of a gastric affliction, possibly perforated gastric ulcers. Philip made his living by prospecting for mica and, as opportunity arose, by selling toys and trinkets such as explosive (so he said) suppositories to amuse the natives of Gubernador Valdares. With his temperament and worldly background he was ideally well qualified to become our children's wicked uncle, an office he assumed with easy grace in his middle years. Although two minutes of his company were enough to have one gasping and clutching for sanity, we all loved him dearly and missed him a lot.

The family returned to England towards the end of the First World War and we lived for a while in a top-floor apartment in the London Borough of Paddington. Futile and ineffectual zeppelin raids were in progress, their jampot bombs causing a dismay out of all proportion to any real harm they did. I remember looking south out of my bedroom window and seeing searchlights combing the sky over south London but my recollection is not accompanied nearly enough by irrelevant detail to assure me of its authenticity. I thus cannot be sure that the scene occurred at all: maybe it was a dream or a vivid description that came later to be clothed in verisimilitude. Who cares, anyway?—it is a common fault of biographers to devote hours of 'research' to verifying biographic details upon which nothing turns.

SCHOOL

My mother (who made all such decisions) wisely resolved that Philip and I should be educated in England, while she and my father returned to Rio. This entailed residence in a boarding school and staying between school terms with relations, especially those needy enough to welcome the little allowance my parents made them to make amends for our huge appetites, our destructive propensities, and the sedatives made necessary by our bringing to an end all peace of mind. Ours, then, was to be the fate of innumerable other children—of Indian and other colonial civil servants, for example, and of all other parents who were obliged to earn their livings abroad.

I do not know that at this time there was any control whatsoever of private schools, either in respect of the welfare of the pupils or the fitness of the staff to teach. All that was needed was a large rambling Victorian house of the kind that had already become unsaleable as a private residence, and a bank loan to make it possible to buy the cheapest possible school furniture, iron bedsteads, rickety desks made from unseasoned wood, and the like. Staff were easy to raise and quite cheap, for unemployment was rife and no qualifications were called for other than those they professed to possess already. My recollection of contemporary preparatory school teachers as a class is that of amiable incompetence. The prep school my brother and I went to first was started by a Church of England clergyman, in collusion with a crooked Irishman who called himself 'Captain Duigan', in a vicarage near Micheldever in Hampshire. The Captain soon absconded with all the school's negotiable assets, leaving Philip and me as the only pupils. The reverend headmaster, far gone in paranoia, soon took to the bottle and did not communicate with either of us in any academic sense, confining his discourse to complaints about Captain Duigan and the ill-treatment he claimed to be suffering at the hands of his housekeeper. All lessons on all subjects were conducted by his good-natured and pretty daughter, who taught us to imitate her own beautiful copperplate, divulged the capital of Persia, and read from Green's *History of England*—an admirable yarn, as many will remember.

Philip and I mixed with the village children and became privy to all their gossip, to which we made imaginative contributions of our own. Our favourite reading was a villainously printed magazine of adventure simply called the *Boys' Magazine*—*not*, indeed not, the *Boys' Own Paper*, which was quite a posh publication suspected of being didactic in tendency and, worse still, tainted with piety. The *Boys' Magazine* recounted the forensic adventures of a detective skilfully named Falcon Swift—a name having the metric structure (tum-ti tum) that was deemed to confer authenticity on any fictional detective: Sexton Blake was another such—a man widely reputed to be a sort of poor man's Sherlock Holmes. I am surprised that Agatha Christie did not see how grievously her own proprietary detective was handicapped by being called Hercule Poirot instead of, for example, Hercule Blanc.

Very early in our schooldays Philip received a cruel rebuff. He fancied himself as a writer and believed he could write stories at least as good as those that appeared in the *Boys' Magazine*. He wrote such a story, therefore, and our simple-minded little teacher was so impressed by it that she resolved to write it out in her beautiful copperplate on pages torn out of a regular exercise book. Accompanied by a civil covering letter this was sent to the editor of the *Boys' Magazine* and never heard of again. We were disappointed and rather indignant and I still think the editor very obtuse and mean not to have understood the situation and waived the requirement (which we did not know about) of submitting at the same time a stamped addressed envelope—thus perhaps recruiting another young hopeful into the world of letters.

The vicarage school soon disintegrated and we were accordingly sent to another boarding school in a seaside

holiday town, Broadstairs, half way between Margate and
Ramsgate. There must have been at least a dozen prep
schools in Broadstairs, some very expensive and très snob,
but the one we went to, 'St Edward's', was comparatively
inexpensive and the parents who sent their children there
rightly did not rate themselves especially genteel.

The first headmaster of St Edward's School was a religious
maniac whose obsessions took the form of improving the
school chapel and making the service as High as he dared in a
predominantly Low milieu. The choirboys entered the chapel
in a slow procession bearing a cross and there were
occasional whiffs of incense. The headmaster was quite
unscrupulous about raising funds, and by exercising immoral
pressure managed to get the boys' pocket money from
them—sixpence or a shilling a week—by representing to
them that their donation would ensure them a future life and
was a better long-term investment than buying sweets at the
school tuck shop. Pious little hypocrites that we were, we fell
for this line of talk and deprived ourselves of an important
ingredient of our diet, calorie-wise.

The headmaster also devised schemes to make the boys
read the Bible all through—though he failed, needless to say.
I did not read the Bible until, lonely in a New York hotel
room on my first visit to the States, I read enough of a Gideon
Bible to be shocked by the way in which characters deceived
and defrauded each other and by their generally un-Christian
goings-on. 'My dear, the *people*!' I wrote home to my wife,
warning her to make sure that such a book did not fall into
the hands of the children.

It was at St Edward's School that my real education began.
At the time and with the confirmation of retrospective
judgement the master I admired most was a middle-aged man
with no hair left on his head except above his ears. This was
the languages master, who was reputed to enjoy a pint of
bitter and to follow the football intently. He taught French
well enough to empower me without further formal instruction
to read French texts fluently, though I never spoke it—which
is just as well because the pronunciation he taught me would

not have been recognized by a Frenchman as his native language. I remember his insistence on our pronouncing as a distinct syllable the terminal *e* of such words as *table* or *entente*. He was specially contemptuous of our speaking as if this was silent: '*tabl*' or '*entent*'. 'No, not like that,' he barked at us, 'say "tabl*uh*" or "entent*uh*".' This Mr Wood also taught English, since it too is a language, and many of us must have had reason later in life to thank God that we learnt straightforward old-fashioned things such as how to write a précis (something that seems to have been dropped from the syllabus because some champion of demotic English ruled that only toffs need to do it), how to punctuate, and how to use quotation marks. Mr Wood construed it as his duty to cause us to become cultured and one of his methods was to require us to learn by heart the answers to a variety of quasi-cultural questions which he put to us in the classroom. 'Take up your pens, boys,' he would say, 'and write down in order the answers to the questions I shall put to you: who or what were Sarah Gamp, Henry Esmond, Circe, Scylla and Charybdis, Odysseus?' None of these should discomfit the reader except perhaps *Circe*—a Homeric sorceress who had the knack of turning people into swine—a trait that caused her company to be less eagerly sought after than it otherwise might have been.

An unfortunate accident deprived Mr Wood of much of his authority over us. Reading to us some lines of Allen Cunningham's

> The hollow oak our palace is,
> Our heritage the sea.

Mr Wood unluckily said 'The 'ollow hoak our palace is', whereupon his odious little pupils laughed derisively, and at intervals throughout the rest of the class one or other boy burst into explosive fits of giggling.

Essays

A most important part of a traditional education in English

was the writing of essays upon a theme chosen by the English master. I remember being once set to write an essay called simply 'Roads'.

I started with the Romans and with a word or two of commendation for the straightness of the Fosse Way; I also commended Macadam for having devised such a neat and effective method of sealing the surfaces of rough stony or gravelly roads. Warming to my theme I said that roads in England were rated first, second, or third class according to the quality of their pavements and the degree to which the exigences of land ownership caused them to twist and turn between private properties.

I felt pretty pleased with my essay but the English master did not. Apparently an edict had gone forth from innumerable institutes of education to say that, to secure high marks in examinations, essays need not say anything or even be about anything: the desideratum that outweighed all others was the exercise of imagination—and how piteously unimaginative my essay on roads was judged to be! My essay would be judged good reading, Mr Wood told me, only by commercial travellers. Why, oh why did I not use my imagination? I asked for some idea about the way in which I should have done so. 'Why', said Mr Wood, 'did you not imagine a road's disappearing over a hilltop and wondering where it might not lead? To a new undiscovered country perhaps—nay, even to fairyland itself.' To this day I cannot imagine how a grown man could have brought himself to the point of talking such drivel. The children were naturally not to know that he was acting under instructions from a literary establishment displaying, as I have since come to think, an almost uncanny grasp of inessentials. I was by no means lacking in imagination: indeed, every night in the dormitory I told the other four or five boys a story—an exciting drama or a comic story, as they pleased, each complete in itself and none therefore the instalment of a soap opera. This went on for about a year. The comic stories were not difficult to compose impromptu because children around nine or ten are easy to please. The dramas, I now clearly see, were simply a farrago of clichés from low-grade detective fiction and, I am now sure, were completely devoid of merit.

Reading

Mr Wood urged us repeatedly to read but had very little sense of the kind of literature that appealed to children, directing us, for example, to *Henry Esmond* and *The Heart of Midlothian*. But we chose our own diet. With children, *that* one reads is much more important than *what* one reads. I was omnivorous and read much as the victims of certain hypothalamic lesions eat, that is, continuously and compulsively. It was mostly trash, of course: motoring magazines, fiction magazines written specially for boys, quasi-adult magazines like *The Strand*, and other magazines like *Titbits* and *Answers*, popular literature published for the newly literate public created by compulsory schooling.

We all read P. G. Wodehouse, that skilful old pro who at a crucial stage in the war created the unfortunate illusion in America that his world of drones and Woosters and country-house life actually existed, which, of course, it did not. My reading also included trade magazines and almost anything one might find in a dentist's waiting room: I always got something from each of them. Thus from *On the Road*, a magazine for commercial travellers, I learned that '365' was the shorthand on the road for bacon and eggs, this being the breakfast had by all every day.

I also read with delight H. G. Wells's wonderfully imaginative short stories and I cut my teeth as a critic by finding fault with the novels of Jules Verne, whose *Around the World in Eighty Days*, although undoubtedly a good yarn, was quite spoilt for me because I could easily see Jules Verne's characters as mere puppets embodying a bourgeois French notion of various national personalities. I can still remember Phileas Fogg, the dour, determined, and indomitably purposeful London clubman, and Passepartout, the witty, ebullient, volatile, infinitely resourceful—and oh so tiresome—Frenchman. I cannot just now call to mind any American in

Jules Verne, but if there were one, it can be taken for granted that he wore horn-rimmed spectacles, smoked cigars, and ate a *chien chaud*.

Although H. G. Wells and Jules Verne were important in a general sort of way, colouring my thoughts and then turning them towards science, the only really informative reading I indulged in was the admirably well-written series of elementary science books published by Ernest Benn. Each *Benn's Sixpenny Booklet* was on a subject such as 'Atoms', 'The Earth', or 'The Stars'.

I was deeply absorbed also by the issues of *The Children's Encyclopaedia*, skilfully edited by Arthur Mee and completely eclectic in its range of topics. I especially remember an article which dealt essentially with the Second Law of Thermodynamics and the 'Heat Death' of the universe that the thinking of Lord Kelvin seemed inevitably to lead to—the world tending at last to a kind of tepid inactivity in which heat was no longer available for the execution of work. I also especially remember on the first page of this article an abominably reproduced inset photograph (from a foxed original, I suspect) of a sanguine-looking bearded gentleman with a nice face, bearing the caption 'Professor Bickerton, who believes that the universe is constantly renewing itself'. 'Good old Professor Bickerton,' I said to myself, 'I *bet* he's right'—a first sign, surely, of my own very sanguine temperament. I read also the *National Geographic Magazine* sent directly from the States, but somehow or other ethnology didn't turn me on—and it still does not: tribal dances are not for me—though I loved the smell of its thick pages prepared for photogravure reproduction and marvelled at its ads for Stutz and other awe-inspiringly large automobiles.

We have all read Sherlock Holmes, of course. Quite recently I was dismayed to discover how badly the stories reread, though on the other hand it was a delight to come again across the tiny little episodes or fragments of dialogue that are the principal cause of Holmes's world-wide following; I do not mean his endearing habit of pausing from time to time to inject a deep draught of cocaine into his veins, but rather such moments as his encounter with an 'ugly customer' who, to impress Holmes, picked up a poker from the hearth and bent it into a right angle. Holmes, it will be remembered, courteously held out his hand to take the poker from him and then, with a slight effort, bent it straight again. Again, did not Holmes once say, 'Watson, what do you make of the extraordinary behaviour of the dog in the night?'?—'But Holmes, the dog did nothing in the night'—'That is what is so extraordinary.' All normal schoolboys love Sherlock Holmes, representing as he did the tradition of unstudied brilliance, showing up with such cruel skill the inadequacy of those bumbling and fumbling professional policemen at Scotland Yard. It is a pity that Conan Doyle lost the opportunity to have Holmes volunteer in a crisis to turn out to play cricket for his county at a moment's notice ('For pity's *sake* Watson, where are my whites?)—and then, probably reeking of camphor, he should have made seventy-five runs before luncheon, thus giving generations of English schoolboys additional reason to revere their hero.

On the other hand we were not really at ease with the works of adventure by John Buchan that our English master more sensibly advised us to read—for Buchan was a good storyteller and wrote a good sentence. I think we early discerned, what adult judgement confirmed, that there is an element of phoneyness in Buchan's make-believe world, a translation into adult life of a schoolboy's reveries and daydreams of heroism and adventure. In Buchan's world, all who are not typecast as villains are brilliant and charming—to a fault, sometimes. For me the world of John Buchan is typified by a dinner party, the members of which, apart from that effortless amateur Richard Hannay, are His Majesty's representative in Boolooland, a High Court Judge, and a surgeon of enormous distinction with long tapered delicate fingers such as the late Lord Moynihan must have imagined himself to possess. Among them too would be the amazingly accomplished New Zealand airman who boasted a score of fifty-nine German aircraft in spite of having only one arm, one leg—and, for all the reader knows, no teeth. Eventually

Richard Hannay turns to the incredible airman and says 'You were in the Passchendaele scrap, weren't you, Jack? I expect you are all wondering why I asked you to dine with me. Well, I want you all to know that the anthropophagi have come out of hiding again and are now working from Malta . . . I am going to need the help of you all in this and as a matter of some urgency. Mainwaring, would you now get as quickly as you can to Valletta and you Carruthers to Famagusta, where you should get in touch without delay with young Ponsonby of the FO who'll tell you where to go next.' John Buchan's world is just as unreal as Wodehouse's but not nearly as much fun.

The combination of religious mania and financial incompetence beggared our little school, which was now taken over by an honest and sporty young Scotsman who in spite of having a withered arm played golf and cricket. The job of caddying for him was in demand because, in addition to getting a good long lemonade in the clubhouse, the appointment carried a stipend of sixpence. In those days for sixpence one could buy a book or six ounces of odonticidal sweets. The new Head also played for the amateur cricket team of Broadstairs which rated fairly highly as a first-class club because there were so many schoolmasters in Broadstairs that they could call upon quite a number of gifted players. I once saw him batting very resolutely against Bill Bowes, one of the fastest bowlers in England, and doing very well.

In due course Mr McVittie came to feel that something was missing in his life; so, to the undisguised chagrin of the housekeeper, he wooed and married a handsome and good-natured young Scotswoman who shared his delight in sport.

The First Sounds of Music

The masters felt—and the boys naturally concurred—that on his marriage the headmaster should receive a present: he was to be bought a portable wind-up gramophone and a selection of records. I remember those records very well. There was a song by Harry Lauder and a rousing ballad by Peter Dawson; a 'laughing record' in which saxophones abetted by some primitive electronics simulated peal after peal of laughter. There was a selection from *No, No Nanette* and a record of popular kitsch including 'In a Monastery Garden' and 'In a Persian Market' by Albert W. Ketèlbey, the former sounding like a reverie in a high-class crematorium and the latter like the kind of music that accompanied the silent-film showing of an eastern souk. In addition there was a recording of the '1812' Overture and, inconsequentially, a very expensive record of Wagner by the Philadelphia Orchestra conducted by Leopold Stokowski playing on one side part of the *Rienzi* Overture and on the other side the tumultuous apocalyptic finale of *The Twilight of the Gods*.

The '1812' Overture would be almost unrecognizable to modern ears because it was played straight from first bar to last. No recording of the '1812' today would be thought saleable unless the passages of what for want of a better word may be called 'music' alternated with simulated musket fire, shots from cannon, the clashing of dustbin lids, and cries of pain from the wounded. I especially remember the record by the Philadelphia Orchestra, because on my first visit to the United States in 1949 I met a very distinguished cancer-research worker, Ted Hauschka, who claimed that he had supplied the reverberant bass notes of those early Philadelphia recordings, and he went on to tell me he had invented a device that introduced a tonally undifferentiated bass boom wherever he thought the record to require it. Its world première was the moment in *The Twilight of the Gods* when the villain Hagen plunges into the Rhine to recover the ring of the Nibelungs—at this point there was an awe-inspiring wump! which made the little gramophone flinch, though as I told Ted it would have been contextually more appropriate at this point to hear a loud splash followed by girlish shrieks of dismay.

I became very familiar with all these records because the headmaster gave the gramophone and all the records to the boys, mainly, I think, out of good nature, but also perhaps because he felt that if either he or his bride developed a predilection for the laughing record the marriage would not long survive. At all events, I developed a private craze for music. Private study at the piano plus some help from my Latin teacher Mr Thomas enabled me to master musical notation. Since I was thus qualified to become a composer, Op. 1 No. 1 was not long in arriving. I wrote some incidental music to *The Merchant of Venice*, then required reading in the English class. My dynamic markings alternated *ppp* with *sff*. *Ma non troppo*, I added, when the school piano in the hall reached the stage at which, having depressed a key, one would lean back and wait for it to come up again: everyone has owned a typewriter suffering from the same shortcoming.

I wondered very much what the composition would sound like and Mr Thomas, quite a gifted sight-reader, played it over for me. I was immensely flattered when at the end of one rather attractive passage Mr Thomas was gracious enough to say 'That's really quite good, you couldn't have written that yourself,' implying that I had copied out some 'real' music from a score. I had done nothing of the sort and was deeply pleased to have been thought capable of having written a passage of 'real' music.

Mr Thomas resolved to educate me musically, having a little gramophone and a few records of his own. He rather daringly invited me into his bedsitter and on one such occasion unexpectedly kissed me on the mouth, mumbling a little shamefacedly 'You will understand when you grow older.' Being completely innocent I was not in the least shocked or resentful; life went on as usual therefore, though I could not help noticing how much Mr Thomas preferred my company to that of an ugly little boy whose extreme fatness had the grown-ups muttering darkly to each other about 'glands'. One of the disadvantages of homosexual schoolmasters is that they can be vindictively bitchy if they feel neglected or slighted by one of their favourites. About a year later the kissing episode was repeated on a dayboy; his father lived in Broadstairs and was determined to make a meal of it, so poor Mr Thomas was sacked. Because I liked him, I was rather sorry about it, and often wondered what became of him.

A Public School

In my time the avowed purpose of the 'public' boarding school was to provide the teenage sons of the well-to-do with education for leadership—to staff the home civil service and to meet the continuing demand for colonial administrators and the foreign service generally. My mother decided that I should seek admission to Marlborough, a large public school in Wiltshire lying athwart the great highway connecting London to Bath and Bristol. It was her choice because her grandfather, I think it was, had himself attended Marlborough. It was not a good choice nor a good reason for making it. After more than fifty years I still feel resentful and disgusted at the manners and mores of this essentially tribal institution.

Because my parents were not all that well-off, I tried for a scholarship to Marlborough from my prep school. I failed, though I did well enough to be excused the common entrance examination that set a national standard for admission to public schools. I have never won a scholarship, though I have done well in examinations requiring that a certain standard should be reached. I can remember enough about my performances in scholarship examinations to understand now why a scholarship never came my way. In the 'general paper' of the scholarship examination for admission to my chosen college in Oxford, I remember vividly that what I wrote was opinionated, superficial, and abominably written: it would have required a superhuman perceptiveness on the part of the examiners to have discerned promise in my answer.

But why do I write about my public school? What can be the interest in the mid-1980s of the shortcomings of a school attended more than half a century ago? I think the interest is much the same as that which might have been excited in, say,

1885 by a Victorian professional man's recollection of Dotheboys Hall.

I entered Marlborough in the winter term of 1928 and was placed in a 'remove' form—about half way up the school—in a junior house* known as 'A' House—an unimaginative name for a school hungry for real or, if not real, simulated tradition. In many ways 'A' House was representative of the school as a whole: dormitories, classrooms, changing rooms, and so on formed the sides of a square surrounding a central well. It was a veritable prison block. There was no privacy anywhere—not even in the lavatories (see below). Indeed, any inclination towards solitude at any time would have been regarded by the masters as evidence of an unhealthy streak in a boy's character.

Public schools are notorious for their traditions. Marlborough was too recently founded to have any authentic ones, so to keep in the swim they had to be invented—particularly a distinctive slang or school patois. Thus the flat cushion that was carried around to soften the hard benches and serve as a wrap-around for textbooks, notebooks, and the like had to be known as a *kish*. There were other obviously factitious traditions too, such as those relating to the number and whereabouts of the buttons which junior boys might or might not leave unbuttoned. There was a tribal initiation ceremony, luckily not worse than tiresome: new boys were each required to stand on their respective beds and sing a song to the other members of the dormitory. No great hardship this: its purpose was no more malevolent than to cause embarrassment and general discomfiture. Beverley Nichols, a popular journalist educated at Marlborough, had told us in his memoirs (written at the age of 25) that he for his initiation had sung, in a clear boyish treble, the prologue to *Pagliacci* in Italian. The mad thought entered my mind that I might be able to entertain the boys by rendering in German

---

* The housemaster was a man chosen by the headmaster for his administrative skills, suitable personal qualities and the kind of example he would be likely to set. In accordance with that ubiquitous tribal spirit, rivalry between houses at sport was encouraged, because naturally the house to which one has been allocated was the best in the school and had to be shown to be so.

the passage from Wagner's *The Valkyrie* in which Wotan bids his heartbroken farewell to his daughter Brünnhilde, though I soon decided that my motive for this bizarre choice would only be that of showing off and being one up on B. Nichols. So I abstained and sang instead one of Ko-ko's songs from *The Mikado*—characteristically Gilbertian in its witless doggerel and gratuitous jibes at elderly spinsters:

> The flowers that bloom in the spring, tra la,
> Have nothing to do with the case.
> I've got to take under my wing, tra-la,
> A most unattractive old thing, tra-la,
> With a caricature of a face.

This song was well received, for W. S. Gilbert was the poet laureate of the class that the boys and their parents belonged to.

The Peculiar Awfulness of Gilbert and Sullivan

Sullivan was a very minor composer who wrote the musical equivalent of Gilbert's doggerel, and Gilbert was much the more offensive of the pair. He was a deep-dyed snob and he knew his audiences were too, so he wrote down to their weaknesses and took cruel advantage of some of their more disagreeable traits. *The Mikado* will serve to illustrate most of his faults. His audiences must have delighted in the opening chorus which is sung by a motley collection of Japanese men who sing a stanza beginning

> If you want to know who we are,
> We are gentlemen of Japan.

At this a titter would ripple through the audience. The idea that foreigners could be gentlemen—and, of all foreigners, the Japanese—would amuse his audience hugely. But there is a darker side to Gilbert. For well-understood demographic reasons too tedious to recount, the age in which he wrote—the age of nannies, governesses, and ladies' companions—was marked by a preponderance of women over men in the marrying years, with the effect that it was an age also of spinsters (in *The Mikado*, Katisha), many of whom entertained a not unnatural wish to get married which Gilbert seemed to despise. This made them the natural butt of spiteful, ill-tempered, or inconsiderate employers and men such as Gilbert, who seized the chance in most of his operettas to raise a sneer about unmarried women that must have delighted his audience and confirmed their estimation of Gilbert as a wit and social critic.

In fact, Gilbert was a card-carrying Philistine and, as we know from *Patience*, did much to create the widespread antipathy to any public display of high sensibility such as the 'aesthetes' were wont to indulge in, mainly to annoy. At Marlborough, and doubtless every other public school, any sign or suspicion of heightened sensibility—even in such a mild form as preferring good music and good books to bad—caused a boy to be condemned as an 'aesthete'. The general atmosphere was thus not only free of any cultural taint but actively inimical to the development of artistic tastes.

One of Marlborough's most disagreeable usages was that which required every boy to have a cold bath every morning throughout the year, no matter what the weather. This practice, it was felt, was so deeply repugnant that it must be salutary and must in any event harden the boys and prepare them for a life in the course of which an event as displeasing as taking a cold bath was taken to be a matter of everyday occurrence. Amidst the romping and general ribaldry of a school bathroom it was quite easy to avoid actually getting into the bath and, in collusion with each other, most of the boys did avoid it. We found that wetted hair and shrieks of dismay before and after a pretence of bathing were a good enough simulation. I was once engaging in just such a pretence when the housemaster Mr Warwick himself came in. It was his duty to set me a good example and I looked on with repugnance as he stepped carefully into a deep cold bath and clasping either side with his hands very slowly and deliberately lowered himself into it. I watched the water close over his chest until it came up to his neck, even wetting his hair. I marvelled at his fortitude until quite suddenly with a flash of insight I realized he was hugely enjoying every second of it. To this day I cannot imagine even to a first approximation what fantasy can have made this unnatural proceeding tolerable, or even agreeable.

I never got to know Mr Warwick at all well but I suspect from what came to be known of his opinions on clean living and the like that he spent much of his time grappling with Satan and that his only form of sexual recreation was beating the boys. Warwick was a simple man and I suspect a rather stupid one. He would have been both incredulous and deeply shocked to learn of the connection between sexuality and the infliction of pain.

One of the worst blunders of the founder of the modern English public school, the Reverend Dr Thomas Arnold, was to advocate a system of delegating a large amount of authority to the boys themselves. This innovation was mistaken because boys so often abused this position and gratified their propensity to bully. In 'A' House three monitors instituted a reign of terror in the common classroom where they sat at a desk in the middle of the room calling out the younger boys one by one and interrogating them in a hostile way to find some reason for hitting them smartly over the knuckles with an instrument they called a 'shillelagh'. This could inflict painful blows, particularly if boys had chilblains—as many of them did, since apart from a quite inadequate open fire in the common classroom I do not recollect that there was any heating at all in 'A' House. When it came to my turn to be summoned before the tribunal, I was asked in a menacing tone 'You're a Jew, aren't you, Medawar?'—with a bang on the knuckles. 'Why don't you admit you're a Jew?'—more bangs. I explained I was not Jewish but of Arabic extraction. No one with any worldly understanding need be told that Marlborough was deeply and solidly anti-Semitic: these boys grew up and as Tory voters in due course joined the Anglo-German fellowship that rated Adolf Hitler not such a bad chap after all but rather a good bulwark against communism.

Pakistanis and Jews

The youths and adults who in my boyhood were anti-Semitic are represented today in England especially by 'Paki-bashers'—people who despise and furiously resent Pakistanis and Indians. The reasons for these two forms of bitter racism are clearly cognate: the Pakistanis look different from native English people, they stick together and often help each other, and—worst offence of all—many of them have become well-to-do through their tireless hard work and general proficiency at carrying out the services they provide. No wonder they arouse furious resentment.

The senior House 'B2' to which I proceeded in the ordinary course of events after spending a year in 'A' house was in no way an improvement on it, being of exactly the same prison-block design: the housemaster, a Mr Maclean, was as stupid and undistinguished as Mr Warwick and every bit as unaware of the petty tyrannies and cruelties that abounded in his House. Stark insensibility was probably not the whole answer: more likely it was a feeling that it was part of the boys' upbringing to contend with cruelty and hardship—it would make men of them. Certainly it would be most injudicious, it was felt, for a housemaster to interfere.

Mr Maclean felt it to be his duty to impart the facts of life to the boys in his House, though it was a subject upon which he was almost certainly less well informed than they were. When the time came for my own initiation we sat in his study facing each other uneasily in armchairs. Mr Maclean broke the silence by saying rather unexpectedly 'Do you know the difference between a bull and a bullock?' 'Yes', I replied and the interview was at an end: he must have felt he had done his duty.

Mr Maclean must have been an extraordinarily bad driver, because on one very cold winter's day he ventured out with his car at a time when any prudent man not obliged to travel would have stayed at home, for the countryside was sheathed in ice. His car must have skidded down a lane that ended in the bridge over the local river. It crashed through a parapet of the bridge, which was much too flimsy to restrain it, and plunged into the river, where Mr Maclean lost his life. 'Silly bloody fool', said the boys, except for the one or two who simulated dismay and sorrow and went around with long faces that impressed no one. The general reaction was one of complete indifference: Maclean had done nothing to earn our affection or respect. We were anxious, though, about his successor, and when the Headmaster came to tell us that he was to be succeeded by Mr Warwick, whose unfitness for the office was of course already known to me, I passed my knowledge on.

J. V. L. Godefroy

John Vincent Laborde Godefroy, known to everyone—with boyish disregard of the sensibilities of the pious—as God, was my closest friend at school. Our relationship was in no way sentimental but founded solidly upon our common love of opera. When we reached the degree of seniority that entitled us to the use of a private study we listened rapt to opera broadcasts from Rome on a small primitive radio set (a 'crystal set') that God had rigged up in his study. Our joy began when a judicious twiddling of dials brought us the beautifully modulated voice of a lady announcer: '*Radio Roma Napoli. Transmissione dell'opera Rigoletto: opera in tre atti di Francesco Piave, musica di Giuseppi Verdi. Edizione Ricordi . . . Personaggi . . . Atto primo . . .*'

Then we were away. Our enjoyment of opera was not merely passive; we ourselves performed. God, an extremely powerful young man with a chest like a barrel, had cultivated a powerful and penetrating falsetto that had put the great *spinto* roles within his power, notably that of Aida herself. I myself, the possessor of a raucous baritone, lacking all beauty of intonation, opted for the part of Amonasro (Aida's father). God would sometimes enter my dormitory with his face blackened with burnt cork and we would embark upon the passionate duet in which Amonasro denounces his daughter at the top of his voice for declining to wheedle her lover, the commander-in-chief of the Egyptian forces, into disclosing the route of his intended attack on the forces of Ethiopia. Amonasro's thunderous denunciations alternated throughout with piteous *sforzando* (fit to bust) shrieks of mercy from Aida. (God, incidentally, later became a recognized authority on Verdi and wrote a very accomplished book entitled *The Dramatic Genius of Verdi*.)

The audience ratings could not have been more mixed. One boy who later became a Fellow of King's College Cambridge has since told me that listening to the Medawar/Godefroy duo was one of the most terrible experiences he had ever lived through. Well, you can't please everybody. On the other hand, the Reverend Canon Patey of Liverpool Cathedral—a good, genuinely pious man—once told my wife that our performances had opened his ears to the beauty of opera, of which he became a devotee.

One of God's musicological discoveries was that all operatic tunes ever written could be sung to the words 'bun' and 'apple' judiciously ordered. We would sometimes walk arm in arm singing the orchestral prelude to Act 2 of *Il Trovatore* that ushers in the Anvil chorus. It went: bun–bun, bun–bun, bun–bun, bun, apple bun–bun, apple bun, bun–bun, apple bun, bun–bun, bun–bun apple, bun . . . etc. When Maclean inadvertently killed himself by driving too fast down that icy road God was able to use this discovery to simulate the tragic course of events that led to his end. At first came the car's even progress along the road: bun–bun–bun–bun–bun–bun –bun–bun–bun–bun, with occasional warnings on the horn, apple! apple! Then an exciting roulade of buns depicted the fate of the slide down the hill followed by a huge crash—APPLE —as he crashed through the flimsy parapet of the bridge, followed by a succession of solemn legato buns rendering the plainsong *dies irae*.

Godefroy was a deeply irreverent man with a contempt for pomposity and humbug that he was quite unable to erase from his broad, cheerful, and often rather sardonic face. It was an expression incompatible with rapid preferment in life—he never became a prefect—especially in a school in which hypocrisy and humbug were major social forces. He was quite a good cricketer, a steady, accurate, medium-paced bowler, with something of the style of the late Maurice Tate. Here too his career was hampered by his insistence upon regarding cricket as a game, played for enjoyment, rather than as a grim competition in which the honour of the school was at stake. This seditious-seeming attitude of God's kept him out of the first team at cricket, the then captain being in our opinion a prissily pious man.

Some Masters

My overall impression of the masters at Marlborough was of eccentricity. Jobs were hard to get at the time of the great depression and the run-up to it; and here at Marlborough, and probably other public schools too, there was a cadre of men for whom the social pressures that make for conformity and orthodoxy had been suspended. Take Mr Stilton for example, an awkward gangly man, looking like an overgrown boy scout, whose foible was patting and pinching the behinds of boys who came up to his desk for their essays or other exercises to be gone over. When he was not engaged in this pursuit he habitually plunged his hand deeply down the back of his own trousers. There was no knowing what gratification he got from this proceeding, which exposed him to the boys' ridicule and contempt. If, for example, he mislaid a piece of chalk, boys looked at each other knowingly and said 'It's probably up his arsehole.'

Nearly all the masters had some singularity of temperament or oddity of manners that exposed them to the ridicule of the cruel and perceptive boys. The senior classics master was a tall good-looking man in his forties, with a high, domed forehead which was given special prominence by his practice of wearing his hat far back on his head. His carriage and general bearing proclaimed his opinion of himself as clearly as if it had been embroidered on his vest: he was a patrician among commoners, the message ran—a rare spirit, a man of deep culture condemned to pedagogy by the exigences of earning a living. The boys for their part plagued and dismayed the masters. A favourite occupation at lunch in the huge school dining-room where the masters joined the boys at table was to choose beforehand some word such as 'bush' which by manipulating the conversation the master was to be persuaded to articulate. If he did so the boys would explode into peals of puerile laughter which left the master wondering what it was in his conversation that had amused them so immoderately.

Another patrician on the staff was the master of advanced chemistry who had got his Cambridge Ph.D. but failed to secure a college fellowship. He was not a good teacher, because of a weakness for making favourites among his pupils. Another weakness was to imagine himself the possessor of an attractive light baritone voice which he used at school concerts to entertain the boys with folk-songs of a kind particularly vulnerable to the vulgar ribaldry of his audience, who had no manners whatsoever—not even a rudimentary sense of fair play such as might have given the performer a fair hearing.

The Headmaster

The Headmaster was known simply as 'The Master', in keeping with the school's collegiate pretension. Marlborough had had a nationally known Master, Dr Cyril Norwood, so widely regarded for some reason as a great authority on education that the popular press invariably associated his name with pedagogic news, no matter how inappropriately. Thus the caption to a newspaper picture depicting a fire might run 'A serious fire, soon brought under control, caused severe damage to one wing of a residential school in Essex for

well enough however to be admitted as a commoner. It struck me that if I were to go up at seventeen, a year earlier than most people, I would save my parents a year's fees, which would be more than equal to the rather modest sum a scholar would get.

I was not at all proud of my prowess at Marlborough and spent a lot of my time feeling discontented. I looked towards university life as the beginning of a new and altogether brighter era.

A particular cause for resentment and regret at Marlborough was that I was not taught to play games, the reason being that in spite of the almost ludicrous degree of importance attached to them the idea of being 'taught' games would have been considered comic. From the day of one's arrival in the school one was either classified as being naturally good at games or, if not, as a duffer. The former were encouraged, approved of, and given plenty of opportunities to play; the others were disregarded completely and sent off on runs, long jogs, or 'sweats' of 2–5 miles, of which the value to the masters was that it got the boys out of the way and out of mischief, serving at the same time the purpose of causing Satan to keep his distance, for Satan's repugnance to brisk exercise is well known. Later in life, as I recount below, I was greatly diverted by village cricket, at which I should have liked to have cut a creditable figure. But I had never been taught the first thing about the game. For example: when young boys start to learn cricket, the bat is much too big for them and they are tempted to wield it with the upper arms and forearms. At some stage they must be taught that when their muscles grow equal to it the bat must be wielded with the wrists. The same goes for bowling: children sometimes start trying to give the ball life by swinging the bowling arm from the shoulder but they also must learn that the final zip is imparted by the wrist. The mystique of untutored brilliance always prevailed in play as in work: only natural proficiency was thought commendable; that which was done by concentration, application, and the will to excel was rated an altogether lesser achievement. It was a very Tory outlook—and the boys took to it naturally.

Being 'good at games' was to this way of thinking the equivalent of having the kind of natural gentility, nobility, bravery, and so on that a gentleman and *a fortiori* a nobleman would enjoy as his inheritance. This natural Toryism found expression not only in the boys' own opinions, but also in those that they picked up second-hand from illiberal parents. I once made a little collection of their sayings to illustrate the kind of talk that came to be called the 'Tory bray'. For example, when the value of pasteurizing milk was discussed, a boy confidently told me: 'No, I do *not* approve of pasteurization—I'd rather eat live germs than dead ones.' Poor silly little boy! It must not be thought, however, that all public schoolboys grew up automatically into Tory voters. On the contrary, public schools could breed the most revolutionary opinions, for it was entirely possible for a not very bright schoolboy to pass his whole schooldays without ever becoming aware of poverty, hunger, deprivation, chronic illness, and underprivilege. When they learnt of these things towards the end of their schooldays they regarded themselves as the victims of a Tory conspiracy to withhold from them information of a kind already possessed by their more intelligent contemporaries. 'If you give miners baths they only keep coal in them.' I have heard the same remark about the bathless state of Southern Italian peasants—'They will only keep spaghetti in them.' J. B. S. Haldane, who was educated at Eton—which is a different matter—became a card-carrying member of the Communist Party; and one prominent politician in England who had been to a very posh public school, at which he was said to have devoted most of his time to auto-erotic practices, became in due course a pillar of the Left.

If public schools are regarded as educational experiments, then they must be judged to have failed. It is indeed impossible in principle that a successful public school could be brought into being, congregating as they do children of like sex at a time when sexual pressures are more exigent than in any other time in life. This objection was raised at a very early stage in the life of the modern public schools, and was disregarded, presumably on the grounds that Christian virtues, manly piety, cold baths, and physical exercise would cope with 'that sort of thing'. These hopes were not fulfilled. This was as true of Marlborough as it was of all other public schools whose pupils I know. They were founded upon the twin pillars of sex and sadism as, by all accounts, were the training schools for the Nazi SS. I must add, however, that very many innocent boys must surely have gone through their schooldays at Marlborough without at any time realizing the strength and pervasiveness of emotional attachments between boys or the degree to which some housemasters derived gratification by wielding the cane. At Oxford, Old Marlburians had the reputation of being a pretty uncouth lot, contemptuous of the life of the mind and of aesthetic sensibilities. They hardly had a chance to be otherwise.

OXFORD

After my four disagreeable years at Marlborough I entered Oxford University in the Michaelmas Term of 1932 as a commoner—that is, a regular undergraduate student—at Magdalen College, chosen for me because a few years beforehand Dr A. G. Lowndes's star pupil, John Zachary Young, had won a scholarship there. Given my parents' limited resources, I myself should not have chosen such a large and wealthy college as Magdalen turned out to be.

After the rude and barbaric life of Marlborough it was a joy to be now the possessor of a decently furnished private study with plenty of bookshelves and a comfortable bedroom attached. I was looked after by a College servant known as a scout, whose father might have been a scout and whose son might be too. Scouts lost no time in establishing a moral ascendancy over their charges, and on comparing notes with my fellow-freshmen I learned that to each one of them his personal scout had made remarks such as: 'Now Mr Clitheroe, sir, him as had your rooms before you— he *was* a gentleman.'

Almost the first thing I did was to assemble for myself a little library, something made possible by opening an account at Blackwell's—an account not finally settled until I started earning my living four or five years later. I did once pay something in response to a characteristic and rather moving letter from them in words to the effect that 'from time to time Blackwell's found themselves in need of ready money and for this reason they would be very much obliged if the substantial bill which had accumulated over many years might become the subject of my attention, perhaps even of a payment on account'. Oxford scholarship—even Oxford literacy, owes more to Blackwell's, surely the world's finest bookshop, than to any other amenity the University offers.

Bookshops

A really good bookshop is not just a matter of bookshelves crammed with books but, more important than that, of an educated staff who knows what the books are and where they are. It is this clause that at once disqualifies a certain London bookshop that represents itself the largest in the world but which gives the impression of being staffed by unfrocked priests and by amazingly ignorant young ladies who simply have no clue at all where any book is and seem rather surprised to be asked. A great bookshop moreover has a large untidy section devoted to second-hand books and staffed by assistants who, so far from regarding them as a pauper's alternative to hardbacks just published, sympathize with and try to find remedies for the book fever of which everyone who uses his mind is at some time a victim. The assistants, moreover, are extremely careful not to fidget or show signs of impatience when their patrons spend hours and hours turning from one book to another and improving their minds apace while looking longingly at editions they would love to possess—were they not far beyond their means.

In my student days great bargains were to be had, to miss which would cause a lifetime's self-reproach, and I look back at myself with regret for missing a very handsome Baskerville edition of Congreve's plays because it seemed a little over-priced at two guineas; but that was at a time when two guineas could—and on one occasion did—take one to Paris and back again.

Oxford was so full of bookshops, any one of which could house a treasure. A stroll through almost any part of Oxford was a most hazardous undertaking for a book lover conscious of being drawn into each bookshop by an almost irresistible attraction, rather like iron filings in a magnetic field. The nucleus of my library, the first set of anything I ever bought, was Oscar Levy's edition of the complete works of Nietzsche. This was not a very sensible choice, but the thing is I had become hooked on Nietzsche through my fondness, to which I refer later, for the operas of Wagner; and no one can make a just appraisal of his works without reading Nietzsche's two great polemics, *The Case of Wagner* and *Nietzsche Contra Wagner*—which in turn led me to others. Nietzsche is a very dramatic and persuasive writer whose style is heady stuff for an adolescent. He wasn't much of a philosopher, to be sure, and theologians and moral philosophers hated his guts, but his writing is full of unaccountably brilliant insights and his aphorisms are well worth browsing in.

I did not see very much of or care very much for my fellow-students in Magdalen. The people I found it natural to be friends with were those with whom it was fun to argue and share enthusiasms—especially musical ones. A keen sense of the ludicrous was another trait I found endearing, and I became friendly too with fellow-students engaged in enviably interesting pursuits such as medicine. Generally speaking, apart from a few originals and some well-chosen Rhodes Scholars, Magdalen was populated by very much the kind of young men the public schoolboys I had known might have been expected to turn into. All of them seemed to have names like Blitherington-Smith or Yuppington-Brown. Magdalen had not in those days adopted an admissions policy that put intellectual promise in the forefront of the requisite characteristics. Rather they were looking for 'good commoners'—in American, regular guys—who would be sturdy and loyal College men bringing distinction to the College by prowess either in examinations or on the playing field. In the outcome, public schoolboys received preferential treatment. As a class these Magdalen undergraduates were egregious snobs—something they would not have needed to be if they had been only half as distinguished in point of family background, wealth, and general prowess as they imagined themselves to be; but snobbishness is a vice of little men, and nearly all of them were. In my first term I arranged a hockey game between teams of zoological students from a class I was attending and chose the Magdalen College playing-fields for their encounter. The members of the teams were in general grammar-school boys and girls: their voices were therefore of the kind that middle-class taste dismissed as 'common'—a fatal obstacle to social preferment since the class system of Great Britain is based more upon the timbre and intonation of the voice than upon any other characteristic. The discomfiture of my fellow Magdalen students at being obliged to have tea with these common-sounding persons was piteous to behold. One of them who made a career in law took me on one side and asked me how the teams were composed. When I told him, he said that he did 'think they were a pretty mixed lot, you know'. I do not think for a moment he was in any way exceptional, for one of the considerations that most gravely disturbed the typical ex-public school commoner was the question of whether his companions were genuinely gentlemen or not. Even the briefest perusal of the pages of *Punch* from the year 1900 onwards will show that this anxiety clouded the lives of the entire middle class, and nearly all the jokes were about the solecisms and awkwardnesses of persons aspiring higher than what was considered their proper station in life. As at school, inborn intellectual brilliance and prowess at games was admired as a natural outward expression of the capabilities their 'breeding' had endowed them with, but anything that might be achieved by application was rated an altogether lesser accomplishment. I remember that when on one occasion I received a moderate academic distinction, a fellow-student felt his own *amour propre* to be restored by saying to me with a dismissive inflection 'I bet you worked jolly hard for it.'

Colleges are great talk places—and talking I hugely enjoyed, falling naturally into the Oxford tradition of levity and light-heartedness, especially about serious things, a trait that nearly cost me a visa for my first entry to the United States of America, as I shall relate.

The College teaching staff (the 'dons') saw and naturally approved the propensity of the young to indulge in talk, and many of them—by no means the youngest—delightedly joined in. Indeed, every College had one or two cynical, sardonic, and ostensibly world-weary dons who derived the utmost pleasure from dazzling and as often as not bewildering the young with epigrams and aphorisms. Harry Weldon in Magdalen was one such and Maurice Bowra of Wadham another. Conversation with—or rather being received in audience by—men such as Weldon and Bowra was a rather formidable experience and an admirable corrective against any tendency towards complacence or acquiescent conventionality of thought. What was there in it for them, beginners may ask. Why, an exhilarating ego-trip and a feeling much the same as an athlete must get when he turns in yet another superlative performance. I did not become the privileged subject of an all-stops-out, all-turrets-blazing Maurice Bowra performance until as a graduate I was invited to dine at High Table one evening when Bowra had resolved to undertake some pastoral work in Magdalen College, down in the valley of the river Cherwell. I was a good-looking young man in a Latin or Levantine way, getting a reputation for being intellectually bright and thus well qualified to be the target of a Bowra display. It was an exhilarating performance that would have made a firework display seem pallid. Bowra was voluble, but his words never tripped over themselves and he was nice—even fastidious—in his choice of them and even dandyish in the clarity of his articulation. Bowra's prowess as a monologist was greatly envied and resented because of the common belief that it was a manifestation of rapidity of thought and genuine brilliance of mind. This must be so, for no one could speak as Bowra did if his thoughts were of a groping and hesitant kind or if he devoted any perceptible length of time to the intellectual equivalent of heavy breathing.

Volubility has some grave demerits, though. When I was a student the BBC ran a very successful middle-brow discussion programme called the *Brains Trust* in which a London University don, C. E. M. Joad, was a regular participant. Joad was hated by his fellow academics not so much for his obvious intelligence as for the fact that whereas his own name was on everyone's lips, theirs, in their estimation equally deserving, were almost unheard of. Joad had many merits. For one thing he popularized dialectic as an intellectual indoor pastime and established a number of rules of disputation by one or two of his most often repeated figures of speech such as 'It all depends what you mean by so-and-so.'

Unfortunately, in spite of these merits Joad did the academic profession, and intellectuals generally, quite a bit of harm, for in the public mind the image of the intellectual became that of a man who always had an answer on the tip of his tongue. Only put the question, however contentious or arcane, and out the answer would come without a moment's pause for the anxious deliberation an ordinary intelligent man would have thought necessary. Burble, burble, burble, burble, burble . . . Next question please.

It was Joad's manner rather than his matter—which was sometimes quite good—that helped to bring intellectuals into disrepute and to give the word 'intellectual' the pejorative overtones that can still be heard in it.

The Tutorial System

Oxford University enjoys the most costly, most 'élitist', and in terms of staff–student' ratio (1:1) most extravagant educational system of any University in the world: the tutorial system. It is a triumph when it works and a cruel bore for both parties when it fails, which is not a common occurrence.

Within a few days of taking up residence in his College, the freshman was summoned for interview by his tutor—an important occasion which determined what a student was to study, or, in the Oxford vernacular, to 'read'.

As well as choosing the subject and mapping out a course of study, tutor and pupil between them decide the student's level of address: someone who was not deeply interested in the chosen subject and would rather be left alone to play games or indulge in Oxford's social life would read for a 'pass' degree; the aim was to get by if not with honour at least without disgrace and to earn a bachelor's degree. A student of whom more was expected and who was thought to have promise would 'read for honours'—that is, to take at the end of his student career an examination which would be classified according to its merits as a First, Second, or Third. This classification played (and still plays) an important part in shaping a student's future career, for a future employer will know that a First in Humane Letters—Philosophy and Ancient History—is likely to be won only by a man of exceptional intellectual capabilities. This school, known as 'Greats', is notoriously a tough one: others are equally notoriously soft options. A student only reads one school at a time, but can read others successively and secure high honours in them all: J. B. S. Haldane, in some ways the cleverest and in others the silliest man I have ever known, had two first-class honours, in mathematics and in 'Greats'. In addition, the scientific research that in due course won him election into the Royal Society of London was in the field of genetics.

At the very heart of every student's course was a weekly interview with the tutor during which his progress and his difficulties were discussed and so far as possible remedied. A common feature of all tutorials was the writing of an essay on a prescribed subject in the interval between one tutorial and the next. A good half of the tutorial therefore was occupied by the student's reading out his essay to the tutor, who evaluated it partly for its content and partly for its success as expository writing.

The purpose of the tutorial scheme is to *educate*—a process to which the mere imparting of factual information has virtually nothing to contribute; so it is not a matter of private instruction but a dialogue designed to promote, exercise, and enlarge the powers of the mind. As a student grows up, so does the kind of tuition he needs and the character and degree of difficulty of the tasks he is called upon to surmount. A tutorial with a good tutor is an exhilarating business. A good tutor will excite enough respect to cause his student to want to please him and earn his praise, and will be most anxious to bring out his student's every capability and help him to get as good a degree as he is capable of.

John Young was a superlatively good tutor and one of a distinguished Oxford lineage. He himself had been a pupil of Gavin de Beer, who in his day had been a pupil of Julian Huxley's. I have no doubt at all I inherited from John Young a number of Julian Huxleyisms, amongst them an aloofly sceptical attitude towards the idea that there existed or could exist any substance to which the word 'protoplasm' could be meaningfully applied. Julian Huxley's son Francis became in due course my own pupil and therefore his own father's great-great-grand pupil.

I took to the Oxford scheme of tuition and I am quite sure I derived enormous benefit from it. Certainly I was elated when after reading one week's essay for John Young he said 'Yes, you're getting better and better', though I was crestfallen when after another he said 'That's all nonsense isn't it?—but I used to write essays like that myself when I was your age.'

John Young was not my only tutor, but no thought ever entered his mind or mine that I should go to other tutors to study the specialized subjects in which these others might have excelled: to a geneticist for genetics for example, or to an embryologist for embryology. Such a proceeding would have been thought dreadfully provincial by any qualified tutor and an abandonment of the very principles upon which the Oxford tutorial system was founded. John Young taught the whole of his subject, as I did in my turn.

John, however, had recognized and approved my philosophic tastes and accordingly arranged for me to sit for tuition at the feet of Thomas Dewar Weldon, the Kantian philosopher known by everyone as 'Harry' Weldon in honour of a well-known vaudeville comedian whose standing in his own department of life was not less than Harry's in his. Harry Weldon was a great figure in pre-war Oxford—a man whose speech, manner, and address to life profoundly influenced all the young men who came in contact with him. He had a distinctive and distantly audible tittering laugh which he exercised continually to give an edge to or invite concurrence with opinions which were usually comprehensively and un-sparingly cynical. Although politicians and men of war were his principal targets, all high officers of the Church and State were also among them. Everybody's competence to discharge any of the functions they were called upon to discharge was called into question and likewise the probity of their motives.

A course of philosophy tutorials from Harry Weldon was a liberal education in itself. I believe Weldon's writings on the forerunners of Immanuel Kant were good stuff and that he should be honoured for the exertions he must have gone to in mastering their drearier writings. But he was not a very creative or original man philosophically and some of his writing on, for example, politics was really rather disap-pointing. Nevertheless he had a searchingly critical mind and he would not let pass anything that struck him as slovenly thinking. I think his judgement in such general matters as we discussed was often faulty: for example, I think he got the relationship between Ludwig II and Richard Wagner quite wrong and that he was equally wrong in suspecting a sentimental relationship between Nietzsche and Wagner. I have not the least doubt that Nietzsche's attitude to Wagner was essentially one of hero-worship—a trait by no means uncommon in young men who meet seniors with forceful personalities whose work they greatly admire.

I hugely enjoyed Harry Weldon, though he did not join me in some of my enthusiasms—for mathematical logic, for example; and he was not equipped to share my delighted enthusiasm for G. H. Hardy's famous text on pure mathema-tics—an exciting and brightly illuminating book for a first-time reader on the threshold of higher mathematics. (I can remember asking a senior and distinguished mathematician why Hardy's text had this quality. 'The reason is', he said, 'that Hardy told the English for the first time a whole lot of important things about pure mathematics that had already long been commonplace on the continent.') I did think then, as I've often thought since, what a great privilege it was to enjoy a system of education so flexible and so permissive as to make it possible for the mind to grow in the direction of its own natural inclinations.

Generally speaking, British philosophy was in a rather bad way in those days: epistemologists were gravely contemplating tomatoes through blue spectacles and reporting upon what they found, and the Right and the Good were the subjects of lengthy and inconclusive deliberations. It was not until after I had graduated that a young teacher in Christ Church wrote a bestseller that was read with breathless excitement by every student of philosophy in Oxford: A. J. Ayer's *Language, Truth and Logic*, a dazzling and revolutionary work which made known to English speaking readers for the first time the thoughts of 'the Vienna Circle' comprising the revolutionaries of logical positivism, the views of men such as Carnap, Schlick, Neurath, and Reichenbach. It was impossible not to be enthused and carried along by this exciting new movement, though when I later on became friendly with Karl Popper I came to hold a more temperate opinion of the new revolution. (But by then I was already committed to a career in research. Harry Weldon also very greatly admired Popper, describing his *Open Society* as the most important philosophic work of the twentieth century even though written under difficult circumstances.)

After graduation I took undergraduate students myself and considered it about the hardest work I had ever done, though I never taught more than eight hour-long periods in the course of a week. It was hard going for two reasons: in the first place the students were an exceptionally brilliant lot with whom there was not much possibility of idle relaxation, and in the second place my laboratory research was so demanding of time and energy that it was not at all easy to fit my students in during the day, so during one very demanding spell I was obliged to take them after dinner at night: I was also junior enough as a don to be expected to drink port after dinner with my fellows—and weak-minded enough to do so. I sometimes found myself at the end of a very arduous day cycling home to north Oxford at 11.30 p.m. The burden of tuition was one of the reasons that resolved me upon leaving Oxford when I was offered a chair elsewhere.

Although I enjoyed and benefited from the tutorial system, by no means all undergraduates do. Perhaps their expectations are too high; so that a young student of Eng. Lit. feels rebuffed when on being first received by a tutor, probably grey-faced with fatigue and the threat of impending boredom, he does not greet his pupil with a newly minted epigram or a brilliant, searching aside about D. H. Lawrence, beginning—as remarks by literary intellectuals so often do, 'Of course . . . '

Tutorials can be a dreary business if any such disillusionment persists, but it is by no means always the student's fault: some tutors are dull in themselves and a cause of dullness in others; and in some of the lesser Oxford colleges the tutors were lazy and self-indulgent men with no teaching obligations other than tuition, and were often at their wits' end to know how to occupy their time. It is among such as these that we find the virtuosi who know by heart *Bradshaw's Complete Railway Guide* and the batting averages of the principal players of English county cricket teams. Such men hunger for appointment to college offices, especially those that entail plentiful committee work, for attendance at committees creates the illusion of busyness and provides at the same time an excuse for doing no creative work ('I am desperate to finish my piece on Otway and Molière, but the fabric committee is simply eating up my time and energy').

A student in Natural Sciences such as I was is not required to take more than one science subject—in my case, zoology, the best-fitted of all the science subjects to provide its students with a liberal education, partly because of the intrinsic interest—even grandeur—of the concepts that inform it, such as evolution, heredity, and epigenesis; partly because of the qualitative exactitude of the formal study of one of its principal disciplines, comparative anatomy; and partly because zoology overlaps with and irrupts into anthropology, demography, and ecology. In later years I came to take the view that a person who was really good at zoology in the broad sense of the above description would be qualified to turn his hand to most things. Indeed Oxford zoology graduates have at one time or another held such positions as Director-General of UNESCO, Director of the London School of Economics, and Director of the National Institute for Medical Research—an undeniably good all-round showing. Zoologists were found useful in wartime, too—in operational research and policy-making and in reconstructing maps from aerial photographs. Generally speaking, students enter zoology through two portals, and many, especially women, are medical or veterinary students *manquées* who have taken up zoology because of failure to get into the course they would really have liked to have taken. The others are bug-hunters, people genuinely and deeply interested in animals—even those such as spiders not often thought of as intrinsically lovable. With this variety of incentives it is no wonder a zoology class comprises a rather mixed lot.

The programme of studies was not burdensome for we met for an hour's lecture at 9.30 in the morning and spent the rest of the morning in 'practical work'. This most often took the form of dissecting a specimen of the animal that had been the subject of the morning's lecture—a singularly futile proceeding from which I derived no benefit whatsoever. I had very many other much more useful ways of spending my time—in the library, for example, or sometimes attending classes of other schools such as physiology, at that time presided over by the distinguished physiologist Sir Charles Sherrington and an exceptionally able group of colleagues.

In my time the Professor of Zoology was a rather selfish little man named Edwin Goodrich. Goodrich was in spirit a member of the great generation of European comparative anatomists of the immediate post-Darwinian era—men such as Karl Gegenbaur, Ernst Haeckel, Karl Ernst von Baer, and Jan Willem van Wijhe. These were the men who demonstrated the theory of evolution—that is, who provided the evidence from comparative anatomy that soon began to make it eccentric or perverse not to accept the evolutionary hypothesis. Edwin Goodrich was in spirit one of them and to understand his career and attitude towards the science of zoology and how it should be taught, one has to have it in mind that until his dying day Goodrich saw himself as a revolutionary, a torch-bearer, the evangel of the new and exciting doctrine of organic evolution, and felt that the principal task of zoology was to put it upon a secure foundation.

Taking this view, and fired by the kind of fervour to be found in some young molecular biologists today, Goodrich tended to feel that only the study of comparative anatomy in the service of evolutionary biology could be serious work and that no branch of zoology reached adult stature until it could be shown to add weight to the evolutionary gospel. Parasitology, for example, was not deemed respectable until the newly christened 'comparative parasitology' could be used to throw light on an animal's evolutionary credentials, though it was a faint and wavering light to be sure.

The great achievements of comparative anatomy had already passed into scientific history by the time I was a student. One such was the discovery that the little bones which transmit acoustic vibrations from the ear drum to the organ of hearing were made up from bones of the lower jaw that had become redundant in the course of evolution with the reduction of the lower jaw to a single bone, the dentary. Comparative anatomy also revealed that in deep structure all vertebrate animals were segmental in character and that many important hormone-secreting organs were derived from regular straightforward organs whose function had become redundant in the course of evolutionary time.

Historically, these great discoveries had been made upon chordate animals and in particular on vertebrates. These then received the lion's share of the attention, and vertebrates were the subject of Goodrich's only lectures, delivered with the intensity that they might have received from those great post-Darwinians of the nineteenth century. The lectures were beautifully illustrated with blackboard drawings in coloured chalks that made it easy to understand why Goodrich had acquired quite a reputation as a water-colourist.

Insects, the most numerous and diverse animals in the kingdom, were cordially disliked by Goodrich. When in my turn I became a teacher of zoology in his department, Goodrich instructed me to lecture to a class at a moderately advanced level upon the insects, suspecting, I think, that I had no use for them at all and would treat them with the contempt he believed they deserved. In practice I enjoyed the work and think I made it interesting.

There is no doubt that the great achievements of comparative zoology are grand and, abstractly considered, deeply exciting. By the time we became students the revolution had been won and was now a matter of history to be found in the textbooks (one of the best of them being Goodrich's own *Studies in the Structure and Development of Vertebrates* which educated zoologists can still read with pleasure and admiration). The revolution had already become a bore and was well on the way to becoming an abuse as revolutions so often do. In general, I found the zoology course deadly dull but I felt some of the intellectual excitement of comparative anatomy and enjoyed writing papers for my tutor on its classical problems. It was intellectually absorbing to study the whereabouts of the anterior end of the vertebrate head, the relationship between an animal's evolutionary pedigree, its *phylogeny*, and the stages it passes through in the course of development, its *ontogeny*; or, again, the degree to which an animal's endeavours and the adaptations made by it during its own lifetime could contribute to the genetic heritage of its offspring. These problems satisfied my growing taste for philosophic discussion and led me to the discovery of a curious aberration of thought of German origin known as *Naturphilosophie*—a sort of metaphysic of nature which failed (as Aristotle often failed) to draw a distinction between what nature *was* like and what the philosophers deemed that it was, or should be, like.

With the help of John Young and discussions with students of other sciences I slowly became aware of what was going on in the world of biology outside the Ruskin museum of old bones in which so many of our studies were prosecuted—and indeed in which the Zoology Department itself was situated. Proteins were being crystallized and viruses shown to contain nucleic acid; and by generating enormous gravitational fields (upwards of 100,000 times greater than gravity) it was becoming possible to separate biological molecules by their differing specific gravities, and by making use of the different electric charges they carried. X-ray crystallography was beginning to make known the essentially crystalline orderliness of biological structures such as hair, horn, and bloodclot fibres so that the distinction between physical and biological orderliness was tending to become blurred. If he had had an inkling of what was going on, Goodrich would have been quite pleased to learn how much of biological order was anatomical, that is, crystalline in character, and that liquids as well as solids might enjoy crystalline orderliness.

With one exception nothing I learned in the formal zoology classes was of the slightest use or had the slightest relevance to what became the subject of my scientific research after I graduated. The exception was the classes of microscopy and histology run by a specially versatile member of the staff, Dr John Baker, who himself worked upon the fine structure of cells, on breeding seasons, and—much to Professor Goodrich's resentment and disgust—a spermicide for use as a contraceptive agent. The practical classes that went with his course on cytology included practical instruction in the best ways of preserving and hardening tissues intended for microscopic observation, dehydrating and impregnating them with paraffin wax, and then using a precision instrument to cut them into slices of the order of thousandths of a millimetre thick. These very thin slices were mounted upon glass slides and stained with a variety of natural or synthetic dyes to bring out and differentiate the various structures in the tissues. I made daily use of all these procedures when I embarked upon immunological research in a few years' time.

I was grateful to John Baker for his useful courses, and when as a graduate student I occupied a room next door to his I was pleased to be able to perform an invaluable service for him—on one occasion he caught alight and I was able to extinguish him. John Baker's doctor, recognizing a man of rather nervous temperament, had instructed him to take it easy—after every meal he was to relax and smoke a cigarette; so one afternoon Baker was sitting in his laboratory smoking, with an open bowl of absolute acetone beside him (God knows why). The bowl caught fire and in his efforts to remove it he spilled the blazing acetone over his lab coat which was itself deeply impregnated—as the coats of microscopists always are—with 2,4,6-trinitrophenol (picric acid, a high explosive). Baker had the sense at this moment to yell for help so I came intrepidly to the rescue, getting a lot of satisfaction by beating out the flames on him with the flat of my hand. This was not at all a hazardous undertaking and Baker was disproportionately grateful. It was my promptitude rather than my courage which should have earned his commendation, for I was very busy and might so easily have said 'I'll just finish what I'm doing and attend to John Baker by and by.'

My second encounter with Baker was not nearly so creditable to myself. He was writing a review that was to include a brief history of the use of dyes in preparing tissue for microscopic observation. One day he looked in to my room for a casual salutation, and I said to him in the way of which graduate students are capable: 'I expect you knew Leeuwenhoek used saffron as a microscopic stain.' As I suspected, Baker had no inkling of this, for I had only just learned it myself from browsing in the pages of a journal of abstracts of scientific papers which had a small section dealing with the history of science. Baker received this news with consternation because his paper was already in proof, but somehow or other he made room for it—perhaps, as my good friend William Holmes suggested to me, by deleting a short passage of doubtless inaccurate information to make room for my discovery. A little later on I received a rather solemn letter from John Baker saying that he had two reasons for being very deeply grateful to me: in the first place I had in the recent past perhaps saved his life (the element of doubt being not whether he was alive or not, but rather whether or not I was responsible for his being so). In the second place I had preserved him from making, in print, a most egregious blunder (there was no hint of reproach at my having been such an irritating know-all).

My attention to the formal zoology course was, as I have said, desultory, for I derived very little intellectual satisfaction from it. I can remember one day, as the final examination was approaching, John Young asked me apropos of evolutionary lineages in reptiles 'What, by the way, *is* a parapsid skull?' I replied: 'I have no idea whatsoever.' 'Oh my gawd,' he cried, 'I suppose it's all my fault, really, but I expect it'll be all right on the day.' I was as alarmed as he was, because John Young had already told me that if I got a first-class degree I should almost certainly get a senior scholarship which would open the doors to a career of research and teaching. I saw the force of this argument and with the support of my future wife Jean I resolved to get a 'First'; I spent the remainder of my time before the final examination committing to memory a great many things I ought already to have known and, although much of the information came as a great surprise to me, it stuck. I felt adequately informed for the written examination though I made a terrible mess of the practical, a notoriously difficult dissection of which the purpose was to verify a point to do with the evolution of torsion in molluscs, a point it had not entered my mind to question. Certainly if the issue had still been a live one my dissection would not have set anyone's mind at rest. Anyway, I got my First and the way was now clear for me to embark upon becoming a scientist. My position had in any case been partly secured by my having won earlier in the year a scholarship that assured me an income of £200 a year for four years. Unlikely though it may seem today, this income was just enough to live on in a quiet way, for young scientists did not then expect to run an establishment and keep a carriage. It was nevertheless enormously helpful that I also went in for and won a senior scholarship ('Senior Demyship') at Magdalen College with a resulting income of £350 a year—free of income tax, of course—which made me a comparatively well-to-do young man who could afford to buy a car.* A good dinner could be bought for 2*s*. 6*d*., thirteen oranges for a shilling, and a ham roll for 1½*d*. It was not high living, but as the hero of the opera *La Bohème* remarks, one lived. My regular supper at a Lyons teashop was a bowl of oxtail soup containing two scoops of mash. Delicious: it was *la vie de Bohème* all over again.

---

* My first two cars cost £4 and (a superior job, evidently) £5 respectively. When in due course these had to be put down, I paid £10 for a broken-winded and superannuated model of a car of good marque.

EARLY RESEARCH

Over the period during which I was *in statu pupillari* as undergraduate or graduate student we were confronted with no threat quite as dreadful as that with which atomic weaponry now confronts us. The world was nevertheless a disturbingly awful place: the numbers unemployed ran into millions. Anger and a sense of hopelessness were the rule with working people; civil unrest was common and protestors were repeatedly convicted of kicking policemen's feet with their stomachs. In France President Doumer, as his name seems to portend, was assassinated, and dictators who regarded war as a manly and even salutary pursuit made no secret of their intention to wage it upon England and France. Spain became a dress rehearsal for a full-scale European war. Political negotiation and the apparatus of diplomacy were unequal to these demands upon them. It seemed that war was waiting only upon the convenience of the great dictators; but in the gathering gloom we continued to cultivate our gardens very much as we do today.

When the time came for me to begin research I had not a clue how to start. Professor Goodrich had declared that the only apparatus needed for a zoologist to prosecute research was a microtome—the instrument used for slicing wax-impregnated tissues into sections thousandths of a millimetre thick—and a microscope, but this made no appeal to me at all (though I think it would have done had I been able to think of some interesting problem in comparative anatomy that needed to be solved—today I should study the ontogeny and phylogeny of the thymus). The subject that tempted me to flex my muscles was embryology. It was already clear that the causal mechanisms at work in development could not be disclosed by anatomical procedures which in effect were trying to depict a cinematic process by a series of still pictures. 'Experimental embryology' had for many years been not easy to work with—they were full of spores such as those of *bacillus subtilis*, the presence of which spelled ruin to tissue cultures at a time when small bacteria-retaining filters such as are commonplace today in biological laboratories had not been devised.

The next step was one which my training as a zoologist left me totally unqualified to undertake, namely the partial purification and preliminary identification of the inhibitory factor. Malt and grain extracts have a brownish coloration due to plant pigments known as *anthoxanthins* and Heaton had somehow convinced himself that the inhibitory agent went with this colouring matter and reported what would have been an important finding had it been true—that the inhibiting substance was adsorbed by treatment with activated charcoal and could be moved therefrom by treatment with dilute acids. It was when I found that colouring matter removed from activated blood charcoal by dilute acids consisted mainly of salts of iron that I realized it was no use looking to Trevor Heaton for guidance in preparative biochemistry. I accordingly made no headway at all, but I thought that after nearly two years of fruitless endeavour I should write and publish a scientific paper and that someone else might take the matter up. The first draft was a rambling and inconclusive discussion of the possible role of inhibitors in the regulation of growth *in vivo* and the theoretical likelihood that such substances might exist. I speculated upon what the chemical nature of the substance might be and exhorted myself to find out.

Florey read my draft with an exasperation and disgust he did not scruple to conceal. 'It sounds more like philosophy than science to me,' he said and, thank goodness, he recommended me to do it all again. It was a very bad paper indeed but the final product* became a modest and predominantly factual paper that in retrospect I am not ashamed of. Florey, however, an immensely practical man, thought it important that I should not let the matter drop and drew the paper to

---

* 'A factor inhibiting the growth of mesenchyme', *Quarterly Journal of Experimental Physiology*, xxvii (1937), 147–62.

the attention of the great panjandrum of British chemistry, Sir Robert Robinson, Professor of Chemistry in the University; he was something of a genius in synthetic organic chemistry, and had no intention of allowing himself to be distracted by such a minor problem in preparative biochemistry. He accordingly instructed his wife, herself a capable chemist, to look into the matter and find out the nature of what I was working on while he made helpful remarks off stage such as 'There are sure to be carbohydrate attachments: look for them.'

This collaboration did not begin until I had returned to the Zoology Department to fulfil an engagement as a junior teacher of zoology, and it did not prosper, for I was quite unable to make it clear to my chemical colleague that, inasmuch as we were studying a substance believed to have inhibitory effects on the growth of very fragile cells, in a very vulnerable condition, false positive results could only too easily be given by contaminants such as inorganic salts in the media submitted to me for testing by biological methods.

With this collaboration I got nowhere, rather slowly. I still don't know even approximately what the chemical nature of Heaton's inhibitory factor was. I should have returned to it today if my career as a bench worker had not been ended by illness.

I resolved, however, to make use of inhibitory properties of the malt factor, whatever it might turn out to be, in a number of largely theoretical exercises devoted to the study of growth regulation. Experimentation having proved to be unfruitful, I turned to the mathematical study of growth—a sterile pursuit that threw no light at all upon its physiology. A number of theorists (I should have been forewarned of the fact that one or two notorious nature-philosophers were among them) made a great show of deducing from first principles the form that a growth function should take—that is the form of mathematical function which, when suitable particular values were attached to its parameters, would fit the growth curve of the organism whose growth was to be described. Although there was no harm in using a growth equation correlating size with age if the function was treated as a summary of information which would otherwise have to be spelled out in columns of figures, the theorists were at pains to deduce forms of growth functions from a priori considerations, in practice always faulty and probably unsound in principle. The growth curves themselves, moreover, were almost always faulty through being corrupted by curves of distribution that sometimes simulated a curve of growth; they were in reality due to inequalities in the time-pattern of growth because of the heterogeneity among members of a growth population under study.

In spite of these deficiencies and deaf to my own warnings, I thought I would attempt to show how in at least one instance it would be possible to attach a real biological meaning to the parameters of a growth function. I chose the Gompertz function as that which gives expression to the idea that, typically, organisms grow at a rate of continuous compound interest which itself falls continuously by compound interest so that where W stands for size and t for age, the growth function has essentially the form

$$W = W_0 e^{k_1 e^{-k_2 t}}$$

where k_1 is the notional rate of compound interest and k_2 the rate of compound interest at which it declines.

This function has some theoretical attractions and it might be deemed to mean something biologically if one had independent means of ascertaining the value of the parameter k_2—that is to say of ascertaining the rate of decline of the specific growth rate. I thought I might do this to try to demonstrate how in a growth system one might estimate at different ages the value of a property I described by the deliberately vague term 'growth energy'. The growth system I chose was the myocardial tissue of the embryonic chicken's heart that had already been the subject of a growth study by the Russian embryologist I. Schmalhausen. I arbitrarily equated 'growth energy' to the resistance the tissue would show to the action factor tending to inhibit its growth. I had found a use for Heaton's malt factor at last. In the outcome it turned out that the 'growth energy' of the embryonic heart muscle over the period 6–18 days declined exponentially, as many bodily faculties do in the course of time, and moreover the rate at which the growth energy declined turned out to be a fair enough approximation to the rate of decline of the specific growth rate of the heart as calculated from the data of Schmalhausen. Thus I had been able to ascertain by experimental means the value of a parameter (k_2) in a growth function—a piffling enough achievement, but I was pleased to have accomplished what I had intended to do.

The mathematical study of scalar growth began to seem to me such a fruitless pursuit that I turned my attention now to the study of *form*, having been deeply impressed, as many biologists were, by D'Arcy Wentworth Thompson's beautifully written essay on *Growth and Form* (Cambridge, 1917). As explained in my wife's and my philosophic dictionary of biology, *Aristotle to Zoos*, Thompson's method of transformations represents changes of shape in growth or evolution in a purely topographical way by showing how an ordinary rectangular (cartesian) grid has to be transformed in order to bring about the transformation that actually occurred in the organism under investigation. Using tissue cultures as theoretical organisms, I was able to put D'Arcy Thompson's method on an analytical footing by ascertaining the 'mapping function' that would transform the normally circular outline of growth in tissue cultures into the variously oblate and prolate forms they would take if grown in a diffusion gradient of Heaton's inhibitory factor or alternatively in a gradient of the growth-enhancing substances such as are found in embryo juices. This exercise did not, however, in any way remove the other objection that can be levelled against D'Arcy Thompson's method, namely that he represented a cinematic process of change of shape by a series of still pictures. D'Arcy Thompson's method would therefore have to be put into motion as if turning a sequence of lantern slides into a movie film. Accordingly I taught myself from suitable textbooks the method of continuous parameter transformations. As explained in *Aristotle to Zoos*, the way to put a transformation into motion is to cause the parameters of the mapping functions that specify the transformation to vary with dependence on age. To illustrate the method I chose some very old data of Stratz's figured by D'Arcy Thompson showing the outline shape of a human being from foetal until adult life.* It is not a good paper, because although the method of continuous parameter transformations is the right one, my application of it considered as an exercise in curve-fitting was very faulty, as Dr Frank Yates once took pleasure in pointing out.

Still being badgered by John Young to take a D.Phil. degree, the time soon came for me to put my findings together and write a thesis which I formally submitted for examination. If the examiners should approve of it I should be empowered to supplicate for the award of a D.Phil. degree (I am using Oxford academic lingo). The examiners appointed to study and recommend on my thesis were the then Professor of Biochemistry in Oxford, Professor Peters, and Dr Joseph Needham in Cambridge. The first was an austere representative of a great generation of biochemists, the greatest of whom was Hans Adolf Krebs. These were men who, incredibly, worked out the pathways of cellular metabolism by direct chemical analysis—that is, without the use of radioactive tracers which would be used as a matter of course today. The other examiner, Needham, was at the time, I think, the Reader in biochemistry in the University of Cambridge, and essentially an embryologist who became an authority on the history of science in China. Rudolph Peters told John Young uneasily that he thought my thesis was 'a bit theoretical', so it must have been Joseph Needham to whom I owe the verdict that empowered me to supplicate for my D.Phil.

I decided, however, not to do so. The degree served no useful purpose and cost, I learned, as much as it cost in those days to have an appendectomy. Having just had the latter as a matter of urgency I thought that to have both would border on self-indulgence, so I remained a plain Mister until I

---

* P. B. Medawar, 'The shape of the human being as a function of time', *Proceedings of the Royal Society Bulletin*, cxxxii (1944), 133–41.

became a Prof. My thesis reposes in the library of the Sir William Dunn School of Pathology, where a casual reader may still take it down, read, and marvel that such a slender and in many ways jejune document could have been rewarded by a doctorate. Such a reader would not know, of course, that by my voluntary abjuration of the distinction it was not.

Honoris causa

In my audacious attempt to demonstrate that human life can persist without the D.Phil. degree I was not arrogant or sanguine enough to be sustained by the thought that one day I should have more doctorates than I knew what to do with. A doctorate *honoris causa* 'is something your friends do for you'. Lord Zuckerman intimated to me that it was a little vulgar to accept every honorary degree that was offered, but then he was not playing, as I am, the diverting indoor pastime of trying to secure an alphabetic full house of doctorates. The current state of play is as follows: Alberta, Aston, Birmingham, Brazil, British Columbia, Brussels, Cambridge, Chicago, Dalhousie, Dundee, Exeter, Florida (South), Gustavus Adolphus, Harvard, Kingston-on-Hull, Liège, London, Oxford (honourable but not honorary), Queen's University Glasgow, Southampton, Washington St Louis, Washington Seattle. Purists (or as I prefer to call them, pedants) may object to my counting Exeter against the antepenultimate letter of the alphabet, and shrewd observers will have observed that Yale and Zimbabwe are unaccountably dragging their feet.

A principal incentive to accept honorary degrees is not, as many people think, vanity but rather that the conferment of a degree is almost always accompanied by an enjoyable party to which one can add the fun of meeting the other honorary graduands, particularly if their work is very different from one's own. There is a catch, though: and persons wrestling on their knees in seeking guidance about whether or not to accept an honorary degree should be warned that the offer of a degree is often accompanied by a civil request that the graduand should address the populace on behalf of all the honorary graduates, finding a few halting words to say what a splendid place the university is and how deeply honoured the honorary graduands are to have joined the ranks of its alumni. When I was receiving an honorary degree at Hull University in company with the sculptor Henry Moore, the Vice-Chancellor had asked me if I would be good enough to say 'just a very few words' after luncheon on behalf of the honorary graduates. I accordingly tiptoed up behind Henry Moore and said to him 'Mr Moore, the Vice-Chancellor presents his compliments, and would you be kind enough to say just a very few words after luncheon on behalf of the honorary graduates?' The great man stopped, turned fully round towards me, with his blue eyes blazing: 'No I bloody well would not' he said in strong Yorkshire, so I did not have to press the matter.

At Harvard University I received an honorary doctorate in company with Mother Theresa and Mr Tennessee Williams. On this occasion the conferment of degrees was followed by an enormously populous cocktail party at which it seemed extremely unlikely that it would be possible to get a drink without a delay that might easily imperil life. I had attended in a wheelchair propelled by my wife. Mother Theresa, seeing this rather touching spectacle, walked over to me and without further ado blessed me, not at all perfunctorily but in the deeply earnest way that I believe to be characteristic of her. When she withdrew Mr Williams hoved into view: 'Mr Williams,' I said, 'Mother Theresa has just blessed me: what are you going to do for me?' 'I'll tell you what I'll do for you,' he said, 'I'll get you a drink.' It was already clear to all that Mr Williams had fully mastered whatever feat had been necessary to secure drinks. When he had fulfilled his offer, my wife drank at least half, as was only right.

A general atmosphere of mateyness prevails on these occasions which may make the basis of a firm friendship as it did with the architect Basil Spence and his wife Joan. Because of this friendly atmosphere, Lord Boyle did not take it amiss when I said at one degree ceremony that in spite of the wearisome familiarity to him of proceedings of this kind it was important that while awaiting his turn to receive the accolade he should do his utmost to remember to wear an expression on his face, a feat he was sometimes tempted to overlook.

When the Second World War, which Hitler had long expressed his intention to wage, broke out, the Recruiting Board told me it was my duty to continue to teach medical students and where possible to undertake research that might be of service to the medical establishment. I accepted this judgement with great relief though my great height (6′ 5″) and preternaturally flat feet* would probably have saved me from the discomfiture of personal combat.

If I had taken stock of my scientific progress at the point when I decided not to take a D.Phil., I should have been forced to conclude that I hadn't really got anywhere or done anything to speak of, but I had not lost confidence in my ability to do something worthwhile. One thing that was wrong with my research was a faulty attitude, something I attribute to being a victim of a Bad Influence—set by someone much senior to myself, namely Dr C. H. Waddington, at that time an embryologist who later became a geneticist. In retrospect I realize that his address to science was more that which might be expected of a literary intellectual or someone on the fringes of the theatrical profession than that of a scientist, or at all events that of a scientist whose name we still remember. He longed to be taken for one of the avant-garde, a leader and maker of opinion, and would have liked to be thought to have been the man who knit together embryology and genetics—but he was not a good bench scientist such as an embryologist, especially an experimental embryologist, must be if he is to win the admiration of his fellows. These are

* My feet were flat enough to have attracted the attention of the philosopher Karl Popper. Once when he and I were attending a philosophic conference Popper said to my wife 'Jean, does Peter have anything against flat feet?' This was not an ambiguous utterance for the great philosopher, for it was a literal translation of the German 'Does Peter have a remedy for flat feet?'

harsh criticisms and to be just to Waddington I must say that in middle life he assembled and kept together in Edinburgh a team of geneticists and biologists who were in general loyal to him and who did creditable work. This was his most important achievement. Anyway, it was my fault, not his, that his example inspired me to do experiments of neither Use nor Light.

Thus back in the Zoology Department I was inspired by the ambition to demonstrate that in a biological system the diffusion of macromolecules in a strongly anisotropic system, such as that represented by a fibrous gel under stress, would proceed more rapidly in one dimension than it did in a dimension at right angles to it. Something of the kind had already been demonstrated in the generation of liesegang rings by two physical chemists, Burton and Bell, who had made the apparatus I needed to try my idea out; but when I told John Young about it he was very scathing and said 'That would be quite a nice little experiment, wouldn't it, and that's what you really like, isn't it—little experiments?' As I had just spent some time on a highly unimportant series of experiments on the rates of diffusion of fixatives into tissues, showing that to a good enough approximation they obeyed the laws of diffusion and did not promote or retard the progress of other fixatives in mixtures, I had to admit to myself the justice of this criticism, resolved to live it down, and in due course did. While I was still working in Professor Florey's laboratory I carried out a number of experiments relevant to the treatment of war wounds, especially burns. Deep and extensive burns that sometimes destroyed upwards of half the body surface posed a new medical problem: in the old days victims of such burns did not really raise a medical problem at all—they simply died—but by the outbreak of war the blood transfusion service was already on a firm footing and the sulfonamide drugs had been introduced, thus putting it in our power to combat the two principal causes of mortality after burning: loss of body fluid and wound infection. If a burnt patient could be kept alive through the acute stage of a burn the dead tissues would be sloughed and leave in their place a raw area filled with a spongy red tissue of repair called 'granulation tissue' through which there was a constant seepage of body fluid. This raw area was highly vulnerable to bacterial infection. It was found clinically useful to apply antibacterial substances locally, in a powdered form, and the question arose of which antibacterial substances would be the least toxic to tissues. I carried out a little survey to test the antibacterial substances most likely to be used and was very pleased to discover that one of the sulfonamides, sulfadiazine, was completely non-toxic, even in saturated solution, to cells in tissue culture which were normally extremely vulnerable to toxic influences. Indeed, it turned out that when sulfadiazine was caused to crystallize in the culture medium, from a supersaturated solution, the cultured cells would clamber on and around the crystal. Epithelial tissues in particular formed tent-like structures using the needle-like sulfadiazine crystal as a tent-pole. I accordingly used sulfadiazine as an antiseptic for topical application in all my own surgical work and it was widely used clinically. Florey asked me to ascertain whether penicillin was toxic or not, and feeling fairly confident that it was not, I am happy to say that I found penicillin passed my toxicity tests with flying colours. I am proud that my name appears in a subordinate position in the credit titles of one of the early papers on penicillin.*

My own introduction to extensive third-degree burns and the grave problems to which they can give rise came about in the following way. One Sunday afternoon my wife, elder daughter, and I were lazing in the garden of the house in north Oxford in which we had an apartment, when we saw a huge two-engined bomber approaching us over the house-tops. My wife quickly picked up our daughter and bundled her into our air-raid shelter which was drier than usual in Oxford, where the water table is only two or three feet down. The bomber crashed into the garden of a house about two

* Abraham, E. P., Chain, E., C. M. Fletcher, A. D. Gardner, N. G. Heatley, M. A. Jennings, and H. W. Florey, 'Further observations on penicillin', *Lancet*, 1941, Vol. 2, 177–88.

hundred yards away and immediately exploded with a fearful WUMP! It was not the German daylight attack we had been told to expect, nor was it carrying bombs.

One young airman was extricated and taken to the Radcliffe Infirmary where 60 per cent of the surface area of his body was found to be destroyed by third-degree burns, that is, burns destroying the entire thickness of the skin. In hospital he came under the care of Dr John Barnes, a colleague of mine working in the Pathology Department who had interested himself in the treatment of burns by irrigation with antiseptic soap solution circulating in plastic bags. John Barnes and the physician in charge were at their wits' end to know what could be done for this patient and Barnes put it strongly to me that I should lay aside my intellectual pursuits and take a serious interest in real life. He insisted, therefore, that I should visit the patient and have some bright ideas as to how he might be treated.

The most obvious treatment, the application of skin graft from a voluntary donor, was ruled out by the fact that skin from one human being would not form a permanent graft on the body of another human being unless the two should happen to be identical twins: this was regarded, and still is, as an inductive law of nature. Only the patient's own skin would 'take' as a graft and grow upon himself.

This conjunction of events had first made me aware of the body's exquisite powers of discrimination also fixed my career as a scientist. I was henceforward to devote the greater part of my time, thought, and creative energy to discovering how the body discriminates between its own and other living cells—'self and non-self' substances, according to Macfarlane Burnet. I understood now how much of my time had been wasted on unimportant projects, intellectual pastimes, and reveries. Laymen and philosophers who have been brought up to think that scientists wield a weapon known as 'the scientific method' may well wonder how I could allow myself to fritter away my time as I did, but there is no such thing as *the* scientific method and I don't regard my own messings-about as any more discreditable than those of a writer who, before writing the novel or play which makes his reputation, spends his time on potboilers and half-finished manuscripts. A scientist who wants to do something original and important must experience, as I did, some kind of shock that forces upon his intention the kind of problem that it should be his duty and will become his pleasure to investigate.

The obligation upon me was now clear: it was to devise some means of eking out what could be spared of the skin left on the patient's own body so as to make one piece do the work of three or four. My first thought was to expand the available skin by tissue culture and for this purpose I paid a number of visits to Rooksdown House, a lunatic asylum which had been converted into a war wounds hospital, presided over by the great plastic surgeon Sir Harold Gillies ('the lunatics presumably proceeding to high rank in the Armed Services', said Harry Weldon, laughing delightedly at the conceit). At Rooksdown House I collected bits of left-over skin from plastic surgical operations and took them back to Oxford to see if I could grow them in tissue culture. Two American pathologists (Simms and Stillman) had shown that the growth of adult tissues in tissue culture, which is normally rather sluggish, could be speeded up by treating the tissue beforehand with trypsin, the agent responsible for digesting proteins in the duodenum. I accordingly incubated small squares of skin in a weak trypsin solution for an hour or two before laying them out on the surface of the semi-solid culture medium. The trypsin, however, had the unexpected effect of causing the outermost cells of the skin to separate from the deeper, more leathery part; these epidermal cells are constantly renewed as they form the resistant protective layer—the cuticle—which is chemically identical with horn and finger-nail. It now became possible, starting with a comparatively small piece of skin, to harvest epidermal cells from it and make them into a thin suspension, a kind of living skin soup—which I innocently thought might be used to seed the raw area, thus causing small islands of skin to spring up all over it. It was, I thought, our duty to try out this promising-sounding scheme and so we did, in spite of being madly frustrated by the difficulty of applying the watery preparation so that it would stay put long enough to allow the cellular seeds in it to settle out evenly over the raw area; but we applied as best we could and found that none of the epidermal seeds 'took' and grew. This was not such a terrible loss, because even if they *had* done so, the flimsy layer of epidermis that would have been formed would not have done the patient much good. Although it might have retarded the loss of fluid from the wound, it would not have prevented the greatest danger for burns patients—wound contraction; this astonishingly forceful gathering-together of the edges of the wound and approximation of its edges disfigured, immobilized, and reduced the blood supply by constricting the blood vessels. Only the leathery layer of skin, the corium or dermis, could prevent wound contraction.

Back at the drawing-board I decided on a different approach—to expand the available skin. Why should we not freeze it to a temperature of carbon dioxide ice (about $-70\,°C$) and by using a special microtome, cut it into slices a tenth of a millimetre thick? The slices might be spread evenly or applied slice by slice with a fine paintbrush over the area that was to be covered. These seeds I thought would be much more likely to 'take' than isolated epidermal cells. This didn't work either, and if these little grafts had 'taken' their use would have been open to the same objections as applied to my epidermal soup. Epithelial cover is simply not enough. Thus in the outcome I didn't do that poor airman any good at all. I believe, however, he eventually recovered as a result of using the 'postage stamp' grafts that had been introduced by a skilful and highly experienced Spanish plastic surgeon, Dr P. Gabarro. These were a compromise between grafts which provided full cover for the wound and the filmy epithelial cover that would have resulted from the use of epidermal seeds and slices: a sheet of skin was cut up into rectangles the size of postage stamps and these were laid in place over the raw area two or three millimetres apart. There is enough of the leathery layer of the skin to do something to prevent wound contraction, and the outgrowth of epidermis from the postage stamps causes them soon to unite into a continuous sheet, just as if the graft had been one that provided complete cover in the first place. I guessed that if one could use what were then known as 'homografts'—that is to say grafts transplanted from relatives or from other voluntary donors—the treatment of war wounds would be transformed.

Although it was not a very original thought, I felt it was important that someone with the right facilities should grapple with the homograft conundrum. I accordingly wrote a memorandum to the War Wounds Committee of the Medical Research Council which impressed one of the Council's principal officers Dr Frank Green, who arranged for my piece to be published in the *Bulletin of War Medicine*. In due course he persuaded me to apply to the Medical Research Council for a grant which would make it possible for me to investigate the problem myself. Green reckoned it would improve my mind out of all recognition if I were to spend a few months working in a burns unit, to be confronted round the clock by the problem that I was to do something about; so I was sent to work in the Burns Unit of the Glasgow Royal Infirmary under the direction of Dr Leonard Colebrook, one of the two very distinguished pupils of Sir Almroth ('stimulate the phagocytes!') Wright. (The other was Alexander Fleming.) The extra income from the Medical Research Council came in very handy because in those days there were virtually no research grants and in the main we bought all our own materials and apparatus. I remember too the pride and joy with which I took delivery of any apparatus I had purchased, especially a neat little angle centrifuge and a torsion balance, both costing £10–20 and therefore well within my means.

It was a relief to be working in the same place as the patients because I had been travelling under difficult conditions, sometimes with a carbon dioxide cylinder and a microtome for skin-slicing and sometimes a Thermos for another purpose. This vacuum flask contained the biological glue I had invented at John Young's request to join the stumps of severed peripheral nerves. The journeys were hair-raising because in those days it was quite impossible to get new tyres and those on my car were at points worn through to the inner tubes, with the effect that I once had three punctures in the journey between my Oxford laboratory and the Birmingham Accident Hospital. One puncture caused the car to weave from side to side until it became a matter of life or death to repair it. I stopped by the roadside, removed the wheel and the outer casing of the tyre, and mended the puncture with the kind of kit most of us had used as boys for the tubes of bicycle tyres.

In Glasgow Colebrook and I stayed in a comfortable hotel, travelling to and from the Royal Infirmary twice daily on streetcars. I was attached to Mr Clark's Surgical Unit, where it was my good fortune to team up with the first of the many truly splendid colleagues I have been blessed with throughout my professional life: this was a tall, good-looking, and very intelligent Scottish surgeon, Tom Gibson—who had in fact many of the characteristics that would have made him a good character in a romantic novel with a doctor hero. We soon became friends, and decided that the first thing we ought to do was to find out and see with our own eyes what exactly happened to homografts that differentiated them from autografts. Our first patient was a 'Mrs McK', an epileptic who had received huge burns from falling against her gas fire. The raw area was acceptably clean and granulating freely. Tom and I resolved that we should graft upon her a population of homografts from a voluntary donor together with some autografts taken from herself. These were to be tiny grafts, 'pinch grafts', each cut by lifting up the donor's skin with a fine hook and slicing off the tent of skin raised in this way by a clean horizontal incision through the base. Each such graft was a button only 4–6 mm across at the base. In order to ascertain what was going on we removed one graft from each population at regular intervals and examined it microscopically. I set up my workbench in the Pathology Department under Professor J. W. S. Blacklock (a Scottish Nationalist who took a chair in London when offered one) and made myself responsible for preparing graft samples for microscopy by impregnating each with paraffin wax, cutting them into sections and staining them for microscopic observation. I was very familiar with all these procedures and believed myself rather good at them. Because I could get on with this job instead of—the usual—waiting for ready-prepared sections to be returned from the histology section, we were able to monitor the patient's grafts very speedily. At first there wasn't much to choose between the homografts that had come from a voluntary donor and the autografts that had come from the patient herself, but after a few days the homografts began to be invaded by white blood corpuscles of the kind known as lymphocytes—the blood-borne cells now known to be those that spy out and eventually react upon non-self intruders into the body. It was then natural to ask what would be the fate of a second set of homografts if these were to be transplanted to the burnt patient after she had reacted upon and cast off the first set. My admirable colleague Tom Gibson already had a shrewd suspicion based upon previous clinical impressions that a second set of homografts would not survive as long as the first set and our histological monitoring showed how right he was, for whereas homografts of the first set had enjoyed a period of grace in which they looked very much like grafts taken from the patient herself, the second-set homografts seemed to be set upon and destroyed right away, to the accompaniment of a specially prompt inflammatory reaction and by a general impairment of the healing process normally accompanied by the penetration of the graft by blood vessels.

This was clearly an important observation, and when my period of secondment in Glasgow was over and I returned to Oxford, we resolved to publish our results without delay. They appeared in due course as a clinical research paper entitled 'The fate of skin homografts in man'.* In this paper we propounded the view that skin homografts were rejected by an immunologic process—that is to say by the same general kind of specific adaptive response as that which daily

* T. Gibson and P. B. Medawar, *Journal of Anatomy, London*, lxxvii (1943), 299–310.

leads to the elimination of bacteria or viruses or other organisms foreign to the body. This interpretation, in which the accelerated rejection of the second set of homografts was regarded as crucial evidence, was quickly and almost universally accepted, though it was not yet the orthodox view which it later became. In retrospect it is not at all easy to say what the orthodox view was, but a different view had certainly been propounded by a prominent classical histopathologist who believed that the time-course and the underlying causes of pathological processes could be unravelled merely by histological study, that is microscopic investigations. One such pathologist had propounded a theory of how homografts are destroyed of just the kind Howard Florey would certainly have dismissed as so much metaphysics. It was full of fine talk about 'individuality differentials' and the like but it did not lend itself to experimental testing and so may confidently be classified as so much nature-philosophy.*

Although the patient had been very intensively studied it did not go unremarked that we were building rather a lot upon the study of a single case, and when I returned to Oxford I felt I should study the whole phenomenon of homograft rejection in laboratory animals to see if this renewed study gave results that would be fully compatible with our hypothesis that the rejection of homografts was an immunological phenomenon. Now began the hardest stint of work I had ever undertaken in my life, especially inasmuch as there were no trained technicians whose services I could call upon. I operated upon all the animals, beginning with several hundred rabbits, cutting and staining all the microscopic sections, and photographed them all on the scale necessary to build up a complete documentation. I was obliged to fetch and carry all the animals upon which I worked and to clean out their cages though their husbandry was officially the work of Italian prisoners of war. I did not feel aggrieved by any of this, because like many other non-combatants I felt

---

* Leo Loeb had done the experiment of applying populations of grafts successively as we had—but Loeb's second grafts came from a donor different from the first—clearly an absurdity.

that the least I could do for the war effort was to exhaust myself with overwork. It was at this stage of the war that the habit began of not only working very long hours but of feeling downright guilty if one went home in the evening without a briefcase full of documents to be read before the next morning.

The easiest part of the project was that of devising reliable and reproducible methods of transplanting skin in laboratory animals, and I am pleased that the methods I then devised are essentially those in use today. In the outcome the immunological hypothesis was fully vindicated by these experimental approaches and I published them in the form of two enormously long papers in the *Journal of Anatomy*.* These two papers described an experiment that made use of twenty-five rabbits operated upon in such a pattern that each rabbit donated a skin graft to each one of the others, a matter of six hundred grafts only because one member of the panel died. All the homografts were rejected. This elaborate procedure was necessary in order that I should be able to allocate a certain minimum number to the immunity-provoking factors ('antigens') that were responsible for arousing immunity against homografts in rabbits.

This research upon skin grafting did not occupy the whole of my time. I could not bring myself to abandon my intellectual pastimes and devoted a little of my time to studying the phenomenon of ageing, by which I mean the deterioration that accompanies growing older, and how it can have evolved under a regimen of natural selection. The main lines of my interpretation were widely accepted and first published in a newly founded magazine, *The Modern Quarterly*, and later used in my inaugural lecture at University College London.†

The other intellectual pastime I allowed myself was to

* P. B. Medawar, 'The behaviour and fate of skin autografts and skin homografts in rabbits', *Journal of Anatomy, London*, lxxviii (1944), 176–99; 'A second study of the behaviour and fate of skin homografts in rabbits', *Journal of Anatomy, London*, lxxix (1944), 157–76.

† P. B. Medawar, *The Uniqueness of the Individual*, 2nd edition (New York, 1981).

1. My mother's mother (*centre*) with her sisters, *c*.1905

2. At Oxford, *c*.1939

3. Jean Shinglewood Taylor, 1938

4. Members of the Theoretical Biology Club at Magdalen College Oxford, 1946. (*From left to right*) Francis Huxley, J. H. Woodger, Hans Motz, Karl Popper, John Young, PBM, and Avrion Mitchison

6. During a Ciba conference at Royaumont in France, June 1959

5. Leaving our house in Hampstead with Jean to collect the CBE, 1958

7. The Royal Society medallists, December 1959. (*From left to right*) Alfred Pippard, Rudolph Peierls, Robert Woodward, PBM

8. At a party held by the Ciba Foundation, December 1960. (*Top*) With Macfarlane Burnet. (*Bottom*) With (*left*) Henry Dale and (*right*) H. W. Florey

9. The Nobel ceremony, December 1960. (*Far left*) Macfarlane Burnet, (*centre*) PBM, (*right*) St John Perse, who was awarded the Nobel Prize for Literature, and Eva Klein from the Carolinska Institute

10. PBM receiving the Nobel Prize from King Gustav VI Adolf of Sweden, watched by Princesses Margaretha and Birgitta (*left*) and Jean and Louise (*centre*)

11. With the family reading the Nobel announcement. Clockwise from the left: Louise, Jean, Charles, Caroline,

12. With Jean, 1980 (Photograph: *Sunday Times*)

T. S. Eliot was also present I thought I would amuse the great man by saying 'Mr Eliot, I am going to write down on this little piece of paper in front of me the name of the novel I believe you regard as the finest novel written in the English language—will you write your own choice?' Eliot was pleased with the idea and we each wrote down our choices. He asked why I had chosen mine and we had a chat about what a frightening character the Revd Dr Casaubon was to an academic—the disagreeable pedant who had been working fruitlessly on a topic which unknown to him had already been the subject of detailed investigation by German scholars before him. I was very much surprised by Eliot's choice, however—Nathaniel Hawthorne's *The House of the Seven Gables*. I had not read it and would not have until this day had it not been for Eliot's recommendation. I lost no time in getting hold of it and felt increasingly bewildered by Eliot's choice, for I found no reason at all to think it the finest novel written in the English language or even a superlatively good one. I never saw Eliot again so I had no opportunity to ask him to justify his choice as I had mine.

C. S. Lewis was a great Englishman in an intolerant Johnsonian sort of a way. He overpraised that which was English (such as the music of Elgar, who was well known to stand squarely in a German tradition of music-making); he crudely undervalued that which was not English, having no use, for example, for Flaubert's *Madame Bovary*, which was disqualified from serious consideration as being about a world of which Lewis was ignorant. And as for *Salammbô* Lewis didn't know what people saw in it (not that it was all that clear to me).

Lewis was a Christian of a rather old-fashioned kind: he believed in the God of the Old Testament—in a jealous, vengeful, wrathful God who would punish ruthlessly. There was not much of the spirit of the Sermon on the Mount here; and I remember his speaking with unmistakable satisfaction of the 'night of the long knives' that would follow immediately upon the entry of the Russians into Berlin—sentiments that sounded strange from the lips of a Christian.

Lewis was a great friend of The Hobbit—John Ronald Reuel Tolkien, an immensely learned and charming man with whom I shared air-raid wardenship in north Oxford. It was not exacting work and when a colleague of mine in the Zoology Department complained to a senior officer that the huge weighty overcoats issued to wardens would not be very serviceable in the rain, he was told, 'Oh my dear fellow, you mustn't turn out if it's wet.' I had brought on duty an old bicycle with little mechanical connection between the pedals and the rear wheels. By rotating the pedals at a great pace the bicycle went very slowly forwards as an aircraft might. 'So *that's* how they brought the good news from Ghent to Aix,' John Tolkien said. On one occasion, oddly, the bicycle went slowly backwards: 'that was when they brought the acknowledgement back again,' the great man opined.

Tolkien thought me young and innocent and felt he ought to guide my taste in wine. Sitting next to me at an Oxford dining club he noted with displeasure that our host had provided us with burgundy and not, as was much more usual in Oxford, claret: 'I think burgundy is a boys' drink, don't you?' he said. On champagne he added: 'If you ask me Mumm's the word . . . though to be sure Bollinger won't let you down; nor will the widow.' 'The widow' is the name popularly given by champagne-drinking folk to the marque known as Veuve Clicquot: it is a designation which recognizes and does honour to the empirical truth that in France, widowhood brings out in women latent champagne-making capabilities that they may not have realized they possessed.

My life of teaching and research was gravely complicated immediately after the war by family problems. After the war my mother brought my father home to live in England in a rather gloomy basement flat in West Hampstead. This upset my father who became, or already was, slightly dotty and believed that my mother had deceived him into thinking that back in England, in contrast to Rio, he would see and walk in green fields and hear country sounds—but we knew very well that he would have paid no attention to either had they been around. In fact, my father's dottiness took the form of phases of black and utterly disabling depression alternating with hypomanic bouts marked by delusions of persecution, to which people of Lebanese origin seem especially prone; the French sometimes describe persecution mania as '*la folie libanese*'.

When my father's feelings of persecution went to the extreme of wondering aggressively who had fathered the three children in the family, I realized that I should have to succour my mother and stay with her overnight; so at the end of the day's work in Oxford I would ring her up and in our agreed shorthand would say 'Is he babbling of green fields?' If the answer was 'Eloquently' then I would drive up to London, stay the night, and drive back to Oxford the following morning after the kind of breakfast mothers are renowned for providing.

FLASHBACKS

Granny Moo

'Muriel'—for my mother was such a one—did not trip easily off childish lips, so by a series of meioses she became 'Moo' to her family and intimates and in due time 'Granny Moo'. She came from a genteel English family, near Winchester, and counted a canon of the Anglican Church among her immediate forebears ('There's glory for you!' she would say). My mother's mother was a beautiful woman and her sisters ('the old aunts') were rated beauties too.

My mother was educated at a ladies' boarding school at which, heedless of the risk of bruising the psyche and stifling the creative afflatus, she was made to learn long tracts of English poetry by heart and to enact with the others a number of scenes from Shakespeare, in all of which she remained word-perfect until late in life. I was not at all surprised when one afternoon during a lull in a leisurely amicable conversation, she held herself bolt upright in her chair and wearing a rather stern expression and in an emphatic manner said:

> That you have wronged me doth appear in this:
> You have condemn'd and noted Lucius Pella
> For taking bribes here of the Sardians;
> Wherein my letters, praying on his side,
> Because I knew the man, were slighted off . . .

She would go on rehearsing what was in her mind until a few seconds later she would burst out indignantly 'I an itching palm!' (This is the famous quarrel scene between Brutus and Cassius from *Julius Caesar*, IV.ii.)

My mother got endless amusement from the thought that the last line of Robert Southey's ballad 'The Inchcape Rock', 'Oh Christ, it is the Inchcape Rock', had been made suitable for childish lips by the paraphrase 'Oh dear, it is the Inchcape Rock'. Once or twice when playing bridge with my mother, I would sometimes see a little smile on her face when she looked at her hand and would know exactly what she was thinking, *scilicet*: 'Oh dear, it is the Inchcape Rock'—and I'd know moreover that it was a hand well below average quality. Bridge was her favourite pastime and she played a good hand: and I was very happy to have been able to fix a game for her every week in the last year of her life with the help of obliging friends who soon became very fond of her.

In just one respect my mother was unscrupulous: she deeply hated sewing and was very bad at it, though not nearly as bad as she affected to be. If on any occasion she was obliged to do some sewing she made a tremendous to-do about it, holding and wielding her needle as if it were an offensive weapon, pricking herself repeatedly, and cursing continuously as she pored over her blood-specked needlework. This went on until whoever was sitting with her would say 'Oh *for goodness' sake*, Muriel, pass your sewing to me and let me finish it'; whereupon the needlework was bundled on to her lap before the dupe could realize how completely she had been taken in.

The Theatre in my Time

My mother took the duties of motherhood very seriously and in holidays from the prep school I attended in Broadstairs she felt I should be taken to the theatre—a favourite occupation of hers which this act of magnanimity on her part enabled her to gratify. We saw Shakespeare and very many musicals—the entertainment she herself liked best. Certainly it was impossible not to be captivated by the abounding energy and vivacity of such shows as *No, No Nanette* and *Hit the Deck*. Having something of my mother's memory and her inclination to exercise it, I can and shall rehearse the lyric that accompanied the hit song from the latter:

> Sing Halleluja, halleluja
> And you'll shoo the blues away.

Sat'n lies await'n
And creat'n skies of grey,
But Halleluja, halleluja
Helps you through the darkest day.

My mother and I also saw John Martin-Harvey in—what else?—*The Only Way*. We did not much patronize the straight theatre, just then beginning the general decline which some years later brave spirits such as John Osborne arrested in the nick of time. At that time all the plays seemed to have the same *mise-en-scène*; either 'The morning room of Sir Richard Halliday's country home in Godalming', or 'The same, three weeks later'. Acting too was in a bad way and not only because this was still an age of actor–managers but because of the deeply debilitating effects of the syndrome of snobismus. Acting was divided into two kinds: 'character acting' or 'straight acting'. It was clear to all parties that character acting—perhaps entailing the wearing of red noses and false beards—was incompatible with gentility. Only a straight actor could qualify as a gent: and so far as he could he created the illusion of having stepped over to the theatre after a light supper at his club in St James's, whereupon with only the slightest veneer of make-up he would appear on the stage as Bulldog Drummond or as Ambassador or a gentleman–crook or, of course, as Sir Richard Halliday himself. The theatre could not be expected to survive when these conventions were in force and it is no wonder that we all so much preferred the cinema. In school holidays my brother and I went to a local cinema in West Hampstead every Thursday afternoon and became quite feverish with excitement when the lights dimmed. Torrid romances were not for us: we liked Tom Mix, Buck Jones, Rin-Tin-Tin, and, of course, Charlie Chaplin. Later in life we were both anxious my sister Pamela and our cousin Stella should come to love Charlie Chaplin as dearly as we did, so I took them to see *The Gold Rush*. No outing could have been more disastrous. The two children sobbed through the entire performance. 'Oh *poor* Charlie, what's he going to do?' they wailed.

It was I think St Augustine who first explicitly drew

attention to what a sophisticated accomplishment it is to read in silence, that is to read without movement of the lips and without uttering a sound. I can still remember that audiences in the days of silent movies fell so far short of this degree of sophistication that some people always read the subtitles aloud. This practice was a well-recognized bugbear of the silent cinema but no one regarded it charitably as a psychological necessity.

My mother had also thought it part of my education to go at least once to the opera. I think she may have cherished the hope that one visit would confer lifelong immunity so that I would not feel the need to go again. While I was still at prep school Sir Thomas Beecham was very busy touring with his British National Opera Company, and they had paused awhile to give Wagner's *The Mastersingers* at the Golders Green Hippodrome. It was an opera of which I already knew the overture, the 'feverish waltz' (as Arnold Bennett once called it), and the hit songs. My mother with great difficulty secured two extremely uncomfortable seats in the upper circle. Sir Thomas Beecham gave us the whole works, without the cuts that many producers would have thought judicious for a suburban audience.

I was enchanted all the way home on top of a bus, but my mother remained silent until she exclaimed how extraordinarily uncomfortable the seats were. She was quiet for a moment longer and then added 'And that *dreadful* old man ... ' referring, of course, to the cobbler–poet, Hans Sachs, one of the least laconic characters of Wagner.

I was still slightly dazed and overwhelmed by the opera, although it was all on a small scale—but it was Beecham who was conducting and he was able to draw from the orchestra the last drop of richness and sonority. I also found the story moving and inspiring. I think that Walther von Stolzing was sung by a rather boozy Welsh tenor. His voice wasn't very good, but he was a trouper who loved the part—he *was* Walther for the time being. At this performance the part of Kothner was played better than I have ever witnessed since: when he described the rules of the Mastersingers and the nature of the prize to be awarded for the winner of the singing contest, he bowed and scraped beautifully, as if dazed by the importance of the occasion and his part in it.

I was a good son not only in fixing games of bridge and plying my mother with duty-free liquor when my travels abroad made this possible, but also in visiting her from time to time with a mending box containing everything necessary to mend fuses, replace electric bulbs, realign door-hinges, and generally put right any of the thousand and one things that can go wrong at home. When my father died of a stroke, my mother, relieved now of the very demanding job of looking after him, was very lonely and, as old ladies sometimes do, found solace in the bottle, which did her liver no good at all. Disregarding her protests ('Doctors aren't a bit interested in old ladies'), my wife and I fixed for her to be seen by physicians, and she was received into a private ward in University College Hospital under the care of a very distinguished physician who told me gravely 'I am afraid your mother's liver is quite seriously scarred.' His treatment brought her relief and she became fit to return home; but then, one day when staying with us, she broke the neck of her femur and was obliged to have a hip replacement.

In hospital she was plastered and immobile, and I thought I would tease her. 'Granny Moo,' I said, 'just what would you do if a lion escaped from the zoo and presented itself in the doorway?' She thought for just a moment and said 'I should address it as follows: "O lion," I should say, "eat me first and never mind these juicy looking young nurses—their flavour simply *isn't* what it used to be."'

Granny Moo died at about 85, proud of, doting on, and dearly loved by, her grandchildren.

Father

Clarence Day's father* pleased and amused a worldwide

---

* Clarence Day, *Life with Father* (New York).

readership because he was in so many respects everybody's father. My own father had no such claim to public attention: he wasn't a bit like anybody else's. I was fond of him all right and was grateful to him for doing his stuff in spite of a grave defect of character. By 'doing his stuff', I mean providing a secure home and livelihood for the family and an expensive education for his children. The defect in character to which I refer was one which, in the milieu in which he worked, deprived him of the ability to perform these duties without a lifetime's very hard work: my father was honest and abhorred the kind of sharp practice prevalent at the rather low level of commerce at which he worked. He was Lebanese, a Maronite Christian, and became English only by naturalization in 1908. He remained fluent in Arabic, once astonishing my mother by the speed and vehemence of his denunciation of a taxi-driver in Beirut by whom he thought himself to have been overcharged. And from time to time he enjoyed browsing in the Arabic edition of *The Arabian Nights*, chuckling delightedly at what the literati know from Sir Richard Burton's unexpurgated edition to be a compendium of innocently *feelthy* anecdotes. This was not his favourite reading though; what he handled most reverentially was the theosophical writing of Madame Blavatsky which, in the language of gobbledegook, in my opinion makes the incoherent rhapsodies of Teilhard de Chardin seem temperate (and sane). It struck me as in keeping with his admiration for Madame Blavatsky that he had a number of food fads such as that grapes ('best things out!') made a diet fully adequate to sustain life. He was a strong and vigorous man, nevertheless, and when we played strength-testing games, as fathers and sons do, my father always won. It was not so in my contests with my own elder son Charles who once floored me and, putting his foot on my chest, was able to proclaim 'At last the old bull elephant is overthrown!'

It will be clear from what I have said about his provenance and occupation that my father was not in any sense a gentleman and he lacked all the graces and niceties of genteel speech, saying, for example, 'Pleased to meet you' upon meeting someone he was pleased to meet. My mother, sensible woman, took it all in her stride and made no attempt at this late stage to transform my father into a silken purse—something that would have bewildered and perhaps hurt him.

My father's most thoughtful and generous gift to me was a season ticket to the opera on a visit to Rio de Janeiro during my first long vacation from Oxford.

Opera Nights

The opera house in Rio is a copy of the Opéra in Paris, and the Brazilians, like the Argentinians, commanded such huge wealth that they could secure the services of any singer they chose. In 1933 they chose perhaps the most popular tenor, baritone, dramatic soprano, and high soprano of the day, respectively Beniamino Gigli, Carlo Galeffi, Claudia Muzio, and Bidu Sayão, herself a Brazilian. In addition they brought over Ebe Stignani, then and for many years after one of the world's foremost mezzo-sopranos, and also Alessandro Ziliani, a young tenor with a fresh and powerful voice who sounded like a very young Martinelli: I am very surprised at not having heard of him again. Gino Marinuzzi conducted. It was all a revelation to one whose opera-going had been confined to Sadler's Wells, the Old Vic (where the Carl Rosa Company sometimes performed), the afore-mentioned Golders Green Hippodrome, and rare visits to the gallery in Covent Garden.

The highlight of the season was a performance in Italian of *Lohengrin* with Gigli as Lohengrin, Muzio as Elsa and Galeffi and Stignani as Telramund and Ortrud respectively. *Lohengrin* is a lyrical piece and its smooth melodious cantilena could have been written for Gigli; the swan was punctual and Stignani shivered the timbers as she knew so well how to do. In the games of one-upmanship that opera buffs love to indulge in, my *Lohengrin* was accepted as at least the equal of that fabulous *Rosenkavalier* with Lehmann, Schumann, Olczewska, and Mayr, Bruno Walter conducting. Gigli and

Muzio also gave an enchanting performance of that surpass-
ingly silly opera Massenet's *Manon*, and there were other
highlights too. I had not seen Verdi's *La Traviata* before,
though I knew the overture with its beautiful descending-
scale figure played cantabile on lower strings; what I did not
know was that this was the music of the dramatic climax in
Act 2 when Muzio as Violetta sang her soaring passionate
outburst

> Amami Alfredo,
> Amami, quant'io t'amo!
> Addio.

At this point I wept to a degree which, though it passed
unnoticed in Rio, would have led in England to a tap on the
shoulder and a civil request from the St John Ambulance
Brigade to quit the auditorium. Another memorable moment
was provided by Carlo Galeffi in *Rigoletto*. At the end of Act
2 the unfortunate Monterone is seen on the way to prison
bitterly complaining that the Duke, the author of all the evils
that befell them, was getting off scot-free. At this point the
jester turns to Monterone and says, in effect, 'That's just
where you are wrong, old man. You shall have a revenge, a
tremendous revenge: *un vindice tu avrai.*' In the bad old
tradition of the Italian opera house, on the word *avrai* the
singer could hold and swell the note as long as he pleased,
although Toscanini would have put a stop to such nonsense.
Carlo Galeffi had an enormous voice which by such abuses as
these had been pretty well shot to pieces, but he knew now
what was expected of him. He forced and swelled his voice
into so paroxysmal a simulation of hatred and vengeance that
we were all quite scared.

On the way home from the opera at midnight I left the bus
half way along the Avenida Copacabana and visited the
rather splendid casino where I hugely enjoyed playing roulette,
for which purpose I used 'My System', as philosophers say. I
commend it to everyone: in playing roulette one has one's ups
and downs and I made it my invariable practice to leave the
casino and go home to bed if I was at all up. As a result of this

I was able to demonstrate proudly to my father a wallet full of worthless currency that represented what I had won over a number of nights. My father looked very grave and said that he did not think it would reflect very well upon him as a member of the local chamber of commerce if his son were seen to be haunting the casino very late at night. After the opera season I did not go again, but I did point out to him that it was one thing to have a son who lost all his money at the casino and came back to ask for more, but quite a different thing—and not at all likely to bring discredit on him—if his son was seen to be leaving the casino with a self-satisfied smile and perhaps even an air of affluence.

The Spell of Wagner

I am spellbound by the later operas of Wagner, though some of the men I most deeply respect and admire, such as Karl Popper and Ernst Gombrich to name only two, can't bear the sound of him.

I have known two other very distinguished philosophers who made a practice of seeing a complete performance of *The Ring* every year. The complete *Ring* is the intravenous or mainline equivalent of that which may be heard in the concert hall or on tapes and records. When I became well-off enough to do so, I twice attended *The Ring* at Bayreuth, a theatre in which the audience is seated not down the length of the auditorium with the stage at one end but across the width of it with the stage set, so to speak, in one of the side walls. By an unfortunate decision of Wagner's, the enormous orchestra is tucked away under the stage and sounds therefore rather like an old-fashioned radiogram, lacking the thrilling presence and immediacy of an orchestra in its conventional placing, but it does give the singers a sporting chance to be heard.

Both the love and detestation of Wagner are largely non-musical in origin. His gifts included the power to transport me out of the real world into one of extravagant make-believe. Wagner's later operas and especially *The Ring* cast a spell by which I am enthralled and I once witnessed its working in a quite unexpected way. A brilliantly funny Canadian *diseuse* with a powerful voice, Anna Russell, was wont to give a monologue entitled 'The Story of the Ring'. This comic lampoon of Wagner's great tetralogy was one which only Wagnerites could deeply understand, so it was Wagnerites who made up the greater part of her audience. Anna Russell told with literal truthfulness how the world-hero Siegfried fell in love with his aunt Brünnhilde and formed a union that was undone by the machinations of Gunther the Gibich ('I am not making this up, you know', Miss Russell added).

Musical illustrations abounded until it became musically appropriate for her to play that solemn progression of chords, normally played *piano* by the trombones or the tuba choir, that signifies Valhalla or its most prominent tenant, the god Wotan.

With this Valhalla motif a great wave of inhibition swept across the entire audience: everyone fell silent and looked pensive and expectant. The spell had worked: we had been transported into the magical world of gods and elves, of giants and dwarfs, and of all-too-human beings. Wagner was diabolically skilful and theatrical in his use of *Leitmotiven*, leading motives, when portraying the thoughts and motives of his characters. For this theatricality and because he hated being manipulated in this way, Nietzsche denounced Wagner and there was a break between them.

BIRMINGHAM

At Oxford I had made friends with Dr Solly Zuckerman, the anatomist who had played the principal part in demonstrating that the egg cells of mammals are not added to throughout life, as spermatozoa are, but represent an allocation that is already complete by birth, the eggs being released from time to time in the course of oestrous or menstrual cycles, to be fertilized or not. Solly Zuckerman accepted the Chair of Anatomy in the University of Birmingham of which he became a loyal, influential, and highly distinguished servant. One of his first thoughts on taking his chair was to contrive such other appointments as would make the University a more congenial environment for himself, and to my great satisfaction his first thought on this last score was to import me and my wife.

There was nothing I could very well be but Professor of Zoology—a chair unfortunately already occupied by a distinguished incumbent, Professor Lancelot Hogben, one of the pioneers of experimental biology and the author of *Mathematics for the Million* and *Science for the Citizen*, landmarks in the writing of popular science. Somehow or other Solly Zuckerman had humanely to turn Hogben into a vacancy, and by a mixture of flattery and cajolery he did so: Hogben received a personal chair in the Medical School. The Faculty connived cheerfully with this manœuvre because Hogben was an unpopular man with a real flair for insulting people, which he exercised too often for his own good. In this game of solitaire it was not enough to move Hogben one place sideways unless I could move into the slot he occupied. Solly accordingly arranged for me to be seen by Sir Norman Hawarth, the Nobel Prize-winning chemist who had discovered the ring structure of simple sugars. Solly knew that if Hawarth approved of me I should be made Professor of Zoology with the least possible delay, for Hawarth was the great autarch of the campus before whom all trembled, and was by far its most distinguished citizen.

After greeting me the first thing Hawarth did was to hand me a small test tube containing a few millimetres' depth of a fine white crystalline powder. 'This is type II pneumococcal polysaccharide', he said. He could not have chosen a more felicitous test for me, because having read Karl Landsteiner's famous *The Specificity of Serological Reactions* I was thoroughly familiar with the dramatic story of the transformations of pneumococcal polysaccharides, and I was able to discourse upon the subject knowledgeably and fluently. Hawarth was impressed and not long after I was designated Mason Professor of Zoology in the University of Birmingham, to take office in the autumn term of 1947. I think Hogben must have felt himself a bit hustled, because shortly after I took my chair I received from him a letter containing the phrase 'the Chair of Zoology, to which you were apparently appointed six months before I had intimated my intention to resign'; but anyhow I was soon accepted as a *fait accompli*.

By the time I went to Birmingham I had been in Oxford for fifteen years—and that was long enough, for I was finding the work of tuition increasingly onerous and time-consuming and I had become deeply exhausted. I was influenced too by the furious resentment I felt every Sunday morning at the church bells of Oxford which abolished all thought and indeed all quietude of mind. On Sunday mornings I would cower at my work-table in anticipation of the holy clamour as worshippers were summoned to morning prayer.

At Birmingham there was no ceremony of inauguration, unless one counts the head porter's formally handing me the key that gave access to all the privies on the campus. I was only thirty-two and very green, so I found much in the City and the University of Birmingham to surprise me. I was amazed, for example, at the ready way the members of Birmingham's great commercial aristocracy (the chaps who had made their pile a generation or two back) told me how much they had paid for their shoes, though I had not expressed an inclination to know. These civic aristocrats did not, in my opinion, cut a very good figure in the Council of the University, where they tended to hold the illusion that whereas commercial firms were miracles of sparkling efficiency the universities were muddy backwaters where water hardly ever flowed. Once when I became Dean of Science I had to defend the University against an opinion expressed by one of them—that university lecturers who did very little teaching and produced no research work for about five years should now be sacked. After this disruptive pronouncement, which I had expected, I made an impassioned oration which I got away with by pretending, what they could not deny, that I was quoting Dr Johnson: 'Sir,' I said through the Vice-Chancellor (the President of the University), 'there is no calling in life in which mere incompetence is any obstacle to professional advancement: we are brought into the world by incompetent obstetricians and if we survive we are baptized by incompetent clergymen who will as likely as not drop us into the font; not long after the growth of the mind is retarded by pedants and pederasts . . . ' I had made my point before the nicest of Vice-Chancellors, Sir Raymond Priestley, shut me up. I do not know in what form, if any, my monologue was minuted.

Because of its civic origins the University felt obliged from time to time to give an account of itself to the City in the form of an Open Day, by attendance at which the public could improve their minds. One such was mounted in my first term and I wrote such an unfavourable report upon it that it did not occur again, anyhow until after I had left. The folk who went from exhibit to exhibit were not able to take much in, perhaps because they were haunted by the fear that they might miss the free tea which had been billed as part of the proceedings. My own demonstration was of one of the most beautiful and remarkable sights in nature: a three-day-old chick embryo lying out on a bed of yolk with its tiny heart beating away and its fore and hind limbs just beginning to form. One woman saw this exhibit and cried 'It's enough to put you off eggs for life', but one serious-looking man came to enquire whether he might ask a question. This is it, I thought, this is where the bridge is thrown between scientific learning and the public. 'Would you please be kind enough to direct me to the toilet?' he asked.

I very much enjoyed the University of Birmingham which, although intellectuals in the Oxford style were not numerous or prominent, had a bounding vitality of its own, especially in the physical sciences and in engineering. The engineers were, in the main, learned and cultivated people and not, as had been taken for granted at Oxford, men with oily rags stuffed into the pockets of denim overalls, their tuition taking the form of bending over a freckle-faced lad and saying 'You see this wheel has teeth . . . and this one too?—Well, if the teeth fit together it follows that when this wheel goes round the other one must go round too, see?'

In my very first term, I was present at the most disgraceful scene I have ever experienced in all my academic life. During a visit of the University Grants Committee to the Science Faculty the senior members were quizzed about their present performance and their future intentions. Humphrey Sumner (a Fellow, I think, of All Souls), behaved to an embarrassing degree as if his mother had once told him he had beautiful hands. Sometimes they were laid one over the other and softly rubbed and sometimes one or both were laid flat upon the table or were used with languid grace to support a chin or, with forefinger extended, the cheek. I should not have minded if it had not been self-consciously intended to demonstrate the manners of a deeply cultivated man, clearly now out of his element and ill at ease in this rather grimy redbrick milieu. He treated the Faculty, especially the professors of engineering, like so much dirt, asking questions contemptuously and interrupting their answers, putting discreditable thoughts into their heads, and taking quite for granted that engineering was the work of barely literate mechanics and electricians. It was a performance of which, as an Oxford man, I was bitterly ashamed. In a few years' time, I myself served on the University Grants Committee but I had the good fortune to come under Keith Murray, who had both the understanding and the manners to conduct the business of the Committee in an academically fruitful way. When Humphrey Sumner's time came to take his leave of the world, Maurice Bowra could not conceal his glee as he sang 'Sumner is agoing out, lude sing cuckoo'.

The staff of Birmingham University had a lack of deviousness that made all business quicker and smoother; and I was surprised and pleased, too, by the quality of the students, all of whom had been chosen before I took office, not by special exams and personal interviews but on school certificate results. The outcome was most fortunate and I found myself confronted with a bright, keen lot, many of them from one form or another of National Service, and now studying zoology because that is what they very much wanted to do. The women students were particularly bright, mainly I think because girls' schools had not been corrupted by the snobbishness that turned boys' schools away from the civic universities. I enjoyed the teaching side of my duties, but getting research started was not quite so straightforward, for the facilities for keeping experimental animals under first-rate conditions of husbandry were almost wholly lacking and could only be remedied by the kind of administrative subterfuge the English are so good at. I was officially visited by an inspector from the Home Office who supervised the issue of licences that would authorize qualified research workers to perform experiments on animals. This inspector was not at all impressed by the conditions under which I worked, so I asked him to do me a favour by writing a stiff formal letter to the effect that the facilities at my disposal were not such as to satisfy the requirements of the Act, and unless they were considerably improved the Minister might disallow experimentation on animals on the premises, perhaps even in the University generally. Armed with this letter there was no great difficulty in raising the few hundred pounds necessary to equip ourselves with animal houses of an adequate standard.

In this research I was enormously helped by my colleague 'Bill'—Rupert Everett Billingham, who had been my first graduate student in Oxford, and whom I had invited to join me in Birmingham, where he became my close colleague and remained so for twelve or thirteen years.

Rupert Everett Billingham

Bill was a student of zoology who secured the highest class of degree awarded in wartime. This was in 1942, I think—an especially bad time for the Allies. Seeing that it was so, Bill resolved to join the Navy in order to bring the war to a speedy and successful conclusion. This accomplished, he came back to the Zoology Department at Oxford with the thought of working for a research degree and went from one staff member to another to see who would be willing to take him on as a graduate student. I already knew how able he was, having examined him for his finals, and I also admired the resourcefulness and versatility acquired by a naval training. Fortunately the project I put before Bill appealed to him and the deal that turned out so rewarding to both of us was clinched. I was very pleased that he agreed to come to Birmingham with me—and because nearly all my work has been done in collaboration with others I should like to make here a few remarks about collaboration generally—a subject upon which I speak with authority because I have had an unusual number of excellent co-workers.

The rationale of collaborative research is the synergism of two or more minds working towards the solution of the same problem (two or more people working together can accomplish more than the sum of what would have been possible if those same people had been working on their own). It is only in science and technology and perhaps in problem-solving that this relationship obtains: it is not easy to imagine a novel being any better for having been written by two authors, or that a mural executed by two pairs of hands should end up a better work of art than the sum of the two performances. More than that, colleagues enhance the satisfaction of having a bright idea or bringing a tricky experiment to a successful conclusion and they make the setbacks and longueurs that are inevitable in scientific research much more supportable.

Loners don't know what they are missing. Fairly early in my collaboration with Bill an occasion arose that made me recognize the value of a good colleague. I had spent a night sleepless with worry at the fear of having made a serious blunder, in an experiment which really mattered: had we used a skin-graft from an albino guinea-pig where we should have used skin from a white area of a spotted black-and-white guinea-pig? In the morning I explained my anxiety to Bill and we decided to do the whole complicated experiment again, making quite sure that we took the skin from the right animal. It sounds trivial but it was not: had we been wrong, abject letters of recantation would have had to be written to *Nature*, with the kind of loss of face that no one finds easy to bear and scientists less easy than most.

The experiment to be repeated involved the use of a tricky and fickle histological technique in which certain cells were to be impregnated with metallic gold by reducing a solution of gold chloride under certain conditions that included the use of lemon juice. Our success with this procedure in the past had depended upon keeping close to the rule book and not taking short cuts. We got the process going, then, and reconciled ourselves to waiting the requisite twenty-four hours. My nerves were sorely tried by the delay and from time to time I said to Bill 'Why don't we just have a peep at one sample right now? It won't affect the impregnation of the remainder', but Bill wouldn't have it, for it was not in the rule book, and his naval discipline ruled out such a liberty. When the twenty-four hours were up, the results of the experimental procedure, which had worked admirably, to our immense relief proved that we had not been mistaken after all: the cells we had thought were there were indeed so, and we had not deceived ourselves in the way I had thought possible. I greatly admired Bill for his firmness and his quick perception of the stew I was in.

In Birmingham Bill and I resumed work together on the project for his thesis—an investigation of the phenomenon of 'pigment spread', the strange process that occurs in spotted black-and-white guinea-pigs and in such as Friesian cattle. Pigment spread in parti-coloured animals takes the form of a progressive encroachment of pigmentation from the darker into the lighter areas of skin. Thus if a dark skin graft were transplanted into the middle of a pale area of skin it would soon come to be surrounded by a progressively widening ring of dark skin. My reason for being interested in this phenomenon was that I had entertained the way-out hypothesis that the branched pigment-forming cells of darkly coloured skin, the melanocytes, were 'infecting' their analogues in pale skin with their cytoplasmic contents, so conferring upon them the power to manufacture dark pigment granules. Bill and I worked very hard on this problem, and did many, as we thought, highly ingenious experiments—but never an experiment of which the results could be interpreted only in terms of a hypothesis of infection. It was a weary and disheartening business representing a loss of about two years' work, at the end of which I had to admit that the hypothesis on which I had been working was mistaken.

Mistakes

This was not the only mistake I made in my research career, but though I should rather not have made any of them I no longer bewail them or feel sadly diminished as a scientist: all scientists who are in the least imaginative will sometimes take a wrong view and waste time pursuing it. This has to be rated an occupational hazard of the scientific life. On the other hand the scientist too scared to speculate boldly can hardly be said to be having a creative life at all, and will end up like one of those sad, sterile men of letters whose taste is so refined and judgement so nice that they cannot bring themselves to the point of putting pen to paper. When I was the head of a big research institute it once or twice happened, when papers were submitted to me, as courtesy required, that their authors apologized to me shamefacedly for having indulged in some speculation—usually nothing more hair-raising than an attempt to think up a possible explanation of the empirical findings. These misgivings are part of the heritage of inductivism—a form of wrong-headedness I have criticized so often* that there is no need to do so yet again. Of course one always hopes to learn from one's mistakes, and part of the fall-out of the 'pigment spread' exercise was that the techniques we devised or improved upon, such as that of causing the epidermis to separate from the leathery layer of skin, made it possible for Bill to undertake a first anatomy of the pigmentary system of human skin which showed, incidentally, that the pigmentary cells of white and coloured people differ not in number or distribution but only in their respective levels of pigmentary activity.

Bill's and my thoughts soon turned in a completely different and much more fruitful direction as a consequence of a promise I had made when attending the International Congress of Genetics at Stockholm in 1948.

At this Congress I met a bright and friendly New Zealander, Dr Hugh Donald, Head of the Agricultural Research Council's Animal Breeding Research Organization in Edinburgh. We spent time discussing the problems of distinguishing between fraternal and identical cattle twins, the difference between them being that fraternal twins which are merely litter-mates are no more alike, except in age, than ordinary sibs; each arises from a separate fertilized egg and they are sometimes referred to as 'two-egg' twins; whereas identical twins arise from a single fertilized egg which at some stage in its development divides to form two complete individuals—'one-egg' twins. The difference between them is crucial, for identical twins have the same genetic make-up and must therefore be of the same sex, age, blood group, and so on; indeed the same in every inborn characteristic. When ordinary fraternal twins are reared in identical environments the differences between them can be confidently described as genetic in origin. Conversely when identical twins are reared apart the differences between them can be said to be of environmental or nurtural origin. (The importance of the

---

* Peter Medawar, *Pluto's Republic* (Oxford, 1982).

distinction was fully appreciated by the versatile anthropologist Sir Francis Galton (1822–1911), the man who introduced the classification and forensic use of fingerprints—and, unexpectedly, invented the term 'anticyclone'.) Dr Donald was engaged in research on cattle twins, using the distinction between identical and fraternal twins to distinguish the differences between cattle that were genetic in origin from those that could be attributed to different patterns of upbringing; but as Donald pointed out, the success of the enterprise depended unconditionally on there being no mistake in allocating twins to one category or the other, and he demanded to know how he could be absolutely sure of his classification. 'My dear fellow,' I said in the rather spacious and expansive way that one is tempted to adopt at international congresses, 'in principle the solution is extremely easy: just exchange skin grafts between the twins and see how long they last. If they last indefinitely you can be sure these are identical twins, but if they are thrown off after a week or two you can classify them with equal certainty as fraternal twins.' I went on somewhat injudiciously to say that I should be happy to demonstrate the technique of grafting to his veterinary staff if he would get in touch with me after the congress. He wrote to remind me of my promise a few months later, saying that all the twins under observation were being held at an experimental farm about forty miles from Birmingham, and he asked me to visit to put my proposals into effect. I was morally committed, without a doubt, so I discussed the whole matter with Bill and we decided to have a go at it together. We accordingly travelled by car to the farm with the right surgical instruments, drapes, and local anaesthetics. Skin grafting in cattle presented no difficulty and our tests began, but the results were not at all what we had expected, since *all* cattle twins accepted skin grafts one from another for as long as we had them under observation. Some of these twins must certainly have been non-identical because they were of different sexes.

These results were totally anomalous and impossible to reconcile with our knowledge of the natural history of skin grafts in all other animals we had studied. We accordingly repeated the entire trial again and started from the beginning; as we got exactly the same results we had to concede that cattle twins were an exception to the general rule that skin grafted on to genetically dissimilar animals would invariably be rejected.

What then *was* so special about cattle twins? We came upon the answer not through any exertion of our own but by browsing in an exciting-looking book newly published by Frank Macfarlane Burnet and Frank Fenner—*The Production of Antibodies* (1949). Burnet and Fenner described some remarkable findings made by an American agricultural geneticist Ray D. Owen, working under Dr M. R. Irwin in the Department of Agricultural Genetics at the University of Wisconsin at Madison. Owen had found that all cattle twins, whether fraternal or identical, had the same blood groups. Each twin contained a mixture of blood corpuscles that were genetically its own with blood corpuscles that could have come only from its twin. Owen had no doubt as to the explanation: cattle twins had long been known to share a placenta. Before birth, then, the twin foetuses must have been transfused with each other's blood and also with each other's blood-forming cells because the red blood corpuscles of the two types present in each twin must have been manufactured anew during life. Bill and I therefore reasoned that the power of the twins to reject each other's skin grafts must somehow have been subverted in the mutual transfusion that occurred before birth. This state of tolerance was, moreover, specific. It was only from its twin partner that a twin accepted a skin graft; a graft from an unrelated sibling or a parent was invariably rejected by a specially brisk homograft reaction. As Bill and I felt absolutely sure that our observational findings were not mistaken, we lost no time in publishing our results in a newly established journal of genetics.* We were

* D. Anderson, R. E. Billingham, G. H. Lampkin, and P. B. Medawar, 'The use of skin grafting to distinguish between monozygotic and dizygotic twins in cattle', *Heredity*, v (1951), 379–97.

R. E. Billingham, G. H. Lampkin, P. B. Medawar, and H. Ll. Williams, 'Tolerance relieved when we had completed our task: it was very time-consuming and on one occasion very dangerous. The route to the farm was along a badly designed highway with many traffic intersections. One day when we were hurrying to the farm, a large truck crossed our path in the course of taking a turn into a side road. We bashed into the rear of it and turned it right round so that it finished up pointing in the opposite direction. The passenger door burst open and, as if intent on exemplifying Newton's First Law of Motion, Bill continued bowling up the road, but was not too badly damaged. The wearing of seat-belts was not usual in those days, with the consequence that I was knocked about on the face and knees seriously enough to be obliged to suffer at least a week from all my associates' facetious but not ill-natured enquiry, 'What does the other chap look like?' I was detained in hospital long enough to receive, in spite of my explicit protests, an injection of antitetanus serum which laid the foundations of an allergy that once later on very nearly did me in. The police brought a prosecution against the driver of the truck and at the hearing in the Magistrates' Court I learned that its proprietor had frugally replaced a broken front-left window of the cab with a rectangle of sacking so that, being unable to see us, the driver had had no hesitation in crossing our path.

Meanwhile, my philosophic interests continued in a rather unexpected way. Karl Popper, with whom I had become friends at meetings of the Theoretical Biology Club, asked if he might come to Birmingham to discuss with me a personal matter which I recount because it shows him in a creditable and characteristically Popperian light.

Popper was at this time a Reader in Logic and Scientific Method at the London School of Economics, where he had thought that his seniority and the quality of his published work entitled him to be considered for the appointment to a chair. Chairs had become vacant from time to time and Popper had put in for them without success. The question he

to homografts, twin-diagnosis, and the freemartin condition in cattle', *Heredity*, vi (1952), 201–21.

now wanted me to answer with the utmost frankness, was whether there was anything about his manner or behaviour or reputation that stood in the way of his receiving the advancement he sought. As it happened, I had already known that this anxiety was weighing on his mind and for that reason I had discussed him with Gilbert Ryle, with whom I had become quite friendly at Magdalen. Ryle held a position of enormous importance in British philosophy at the time, simply because of the vigour and prosperity of the School of Linguistic Analysis in Oxford which he had played a large part in creating, and his stature was now such that he had more weight that any other philosopher in appointments to chairs throughout the country. What Ryle had told me was that Popper had a reputation for being rather intolerant and overbearing with his students and resentful if their opinions differed radically from his own. In conveying the gist of this to Popper I told him of the terms in which I had protested to Ryle about the injustice of such a judgement; I had told him that Popper was above all else a believer in the fruitfulness of rational discussion—conversely he was easily dismayed when an interlocutor was brusque and overbearing and would not accept his arguments although unable to rebut them. The most sharply critical remark I ever heard Karl Popper make about another human being concerned an arrogant and overbearing biologist of whom Popper said 'Oh yes, I do know —— : he is "unteachable".' I think Popper's visit to Birmingham did something to reassure him, and soon afterwards he was appointed to the Chair of Logic and Scientific Method at the London School of Economics.

Popper is held in the highest esteem by scientists, a number of whom conspired a few years ago to bring it about that he was elected into the Fellowship of the world's oldest and most famous scientific society, the Royal Society of London. I am very sorry to have to report that a good many philosophers are jealous of Popper, pick fault where they can, and find reasons to praise philosophers who put forward views different from his, even when those views are somewhat flimsy. I have a feeling that many lecturers on scientific method are oppressed by the sheer reasonableness of Popper's philosophy, and in taking a different or very critical line they feel that their personal identity has somehow been enlarged. Worse still, it has become the thing for literary intellectuals to pretend that there is something a little *passé* about Popper's philosophy and that he has been supplanted by a number of mavericks and clowns.

In Birmingham I performed a literary duty with the help of a dictating machine and a patient secretary: this was to read and largely to rewrite a most important monograph for the Clarendon Press by the distinguished pioneer of animal behaviour studies in this country, Niko Tinbergen, for whom Alister Hardy had contrived to make a suitable ecological niche in the Department of Zoology in Oxford. This work, *The Study of Instinct*, gave me an insight into ethology which I should not otherwise have possessed and in turn made it possible for me to promote Tinbergen's work in Oxford by writing in laudatory terms about it to the Nuffield Foundation. My letter served as an antidote to the opinion of one of the grant-giving committee. 'Ethology?' he had said. 'I thought that was some branch of bird-watching.' When Niko Tinbergen won the Nobel Prize the Nuffield Foundation kindly sent me a xerograph of this letter. Later on I arranged for Desmond Morris, one of the brightest of my zoology students, to work under Tinbergen for his doctorate, and they soon became close friends.

A Visit to America

It is not widely enough known in Great Britain that the rebirth of science in Europe after the war was very largely made possible through enormous subventions by private foundations and federal sources in the United States. Agents of the great charitable foundations travelled around offering financial help to scientists thought worth backing. The great Foundations and other wealthy sponsors can exercise a most significant influence on the growth of a science, organizing scientific conferences and more informal get-togethers, that keeps the fermentation going and makes scientists in cognate fields aware of it. I especially acknowledge the services of the Ciba Foundation, which greatly assisted the development of the science of endocrinology when it was at about the same stage of development as our own speciality. Scientific academies played their part too, above all the New York Academy of Sciences, which organized and funded big international meetings on transplantation which in due course became the conferences of the International Transplantation Society. In Birmingham I received a visit from Dr Gerard Pomerat representing the Rockefeller Foundation; he put it to me that it might benefit me academically if I were to spend some little time in America. As I told him, it would be a very great thrill for me to spend a few months sitting at the feet of Peyton Rous in the Rockefeller Institute, at that time the foremost centre of biomedical research in the world and in many respects the model of institutions such as the National Institute for Medical Research in London. Peyton Rous himself was the world's foremost experimental pathologist— a man of enormous culture and learning whose great scientific achievement had been to show that a tumour of chickens was caused by a virus.

I explained to Dr Pomerat that as a salaried servant of the University I couldn't simply get up and go, and that I ought in any event to confine my visit to a matter of three months or so, a period during which I should be able to accept an invitation from Harvard University to deliver the so-called Prather Lectures to the assembled biologists. Pomerat approved of my plans and said that the Foundation would make it possible for me to visit a whole number of centres in the United States and make contact with scientists I particularly wanted to meet.

Getting a Visa

Persons educated at Oxford very readily acquire a conversational manner marked by a certain lightness of touch—a dedicated repudiation of *gravitas* or portentousness in all its forms. I picked up this touch and the kind of banter that goes with it, but was never warned that although its use was fine with other Oxford people it should on no account be used in dealings with officials, who are obliged to take themselves seriously and regard jokes on official matters as akin to laughing in church. My failure to appreciate this nearly cost me the visa I needed to gain admission to the United States. The year 1949 was not a good moment in American history. It was at the height of the anti-intellectual movement generated by Senator McCarthy when it was suspected that people who thought at all might easily think ill of America. When the official who interviewed me at the American Consulate in London asked the purpose of my visit to America, I replied that it was to give a number of lectures at Harvard. This identified me as an intellectual, and my longish hair and lean and hungry look probably only reinforced the impression. Then, on being asked to make the formal declaration that I did not intend to overthrow the Constitution of the United States, I was fool enough to reply that I had no such purpose, but that were I to do it by mistake I should be inexpressibly contrite. The official was naturally puzzled and annoyed, but in spite of these misgivings I secured my visa and under the patronage of the Rockefeller Foundation I sailed for America in September 1949 on SS *Mauretania* with instructions to report to my patrons the day after arrival at 49 West 49th Street. I had formed a mental picture of an elegant little terrace of houses of which one, No. 49, would be marked by the complete lack of ostentation characteristic of the enormously wealthy. Perhaps I should have got an inkling of the truth from the fact that I was instructed to report on the 55th floor, for No. 49 turned out to be the tallest building I had until then set eyes upon. It was surrounded by slightly lesser buildings that formed the breath-taking ensemble of the Rockefeller Center. My hosts received me in the friendliest possible way, enquiring after my comfort and my intentions, and proceeded, with the liberality that the name Rockefeller conjures up, to hand out hundreds of dollars. Soon I went to introduce myself to Dr Rous, who took me to the famous luncheon room of the Rockefeller Institute, where over a period of time one could meet a pantheon of scientists whose names were household words in the profession—men such as Dubos, Shope, Paul Weiss, Gasser the neurophysiologist, Colin Macleod and Maclyn McCarty—these last two being principals in the most exciting and revealing biological experiment of the twentieth century, which had showed that the genes were composed of deoxyribonucleic acid.

I had a number of stories to tell in connection with homografts, pigment spread, and twin cattle and was invited to a number of laboratories to give talks. At one of the many dinner parties to which I was also invited, my host asked what it was that had most struck me about America. I knew I should be asked this question and did not know what I ought to say, so I said what I really thought: 'The apparently relaxed ease with which Americans plan and execute the most enormous engineering enterprises.' Our host's discomfiture was apparent. 'What most people say', he said with an air of rebuke, 'is how amazed they are by the number of cars.' I felt doubly reproached because the idea had just crossed my mind of saying in the cockney idiom 'What amazes me is you seem to be completely overrun by all these bloody cars.' Luckily I had already sensed the special relationship between an American and his car that would have made such an answer most injudicious.

Everyone Can Remember His First Cocktail

On Thanksgiving Day Peyton Rous took pity on the young and ignorant foreigner and gave him Thanksgiving Dinner in the Century Club, where I arrived in my sensible English worsteds hot and perspiring—for New York is very humid in the Fall—to find my discomfiture compounded by the heat in the Club itself. Dr Rous asked me if I would like a cocktail and I guessed that he was going to have one anyway. I told him that I had never had a cocktail before, but that I had heard the Manhattan well spoken of, so I would like one of those. A large Manhattan was put beside me and beside that a pitcher containing more than as much again. I liked the taste and being thirsty I drank the whole lot. We went shortly to dinner: turkey and pumpkin pie accompanied by a bottle of robust Californian wine. Not long after, I passed out or rather, as old-fashioned novelists say, 'I offered to pass out.' Dr Rous, remembering that he was an MD, bade me sit down and put my head between my knees. He was himself in a difficult position because being a most perfect gentleman he was suffering agonies of vicarious embarrassment, trying desperately to put me at my ease, but clearly being unwilling to say I had drunk too much too fast. Then a bright idea came to his rescue: it was a sudden and unpredictable allergic manifestation, he said. It was the pumpkin pie: *pumpkin pie simply did not agree with some people.* These idiosyncrasies were among the most puzzling phenomena in the whole of modern medicine, and their explanation was still far to seek. I listened very attentively so that Peyton should no longer feel embarrassed for me, but I could not erase my consciousness of having behaved rather foolishly. I took my leave soon after, having suddenly, almost addictively, acquired a taste for American cocktails which I introduced into our domestic economy on my return from the States. Indeed, I made a practice of serving them at a party we gave regularly at home for the Annual Meeting of the Society for Experimental Biology. At one such party the wife of a very distinguished professor drank dry Martinis as injudiciously as I had my Manhattans. 'Mama,' our younger daughter said, 'why does that lady keep falling down?' The lady came back next day to apologize and collect her forgotten handbag. She was recognized on the spot: 'Oh Mama, *that*'s the lady who kept on falling down.'

I struck one blow for freedom during my visit to America. I was invited to give a talk at the National Cancer Institute, an invitation accompanied by an instruction to present myself before a notary public to be fingerprinted. This I refused to do, explaining on arrival in Bethesda that the information I was going to impart to them would be of no use at all to an enemy. Although the head of the Institute praised me for my stand, the domestic rules obliged him to fine me by withholding the sum that would otherwise have been my honorarium. The National Cancer Institute is thus morally my debtor to the tune of about $150.

Among my other out-of-town trips under the patronage of the Rockefeller Foundation was a visit to Yale where I had the pleasure of being introduced to Dr Ross Granville Harrison, an embryologist of enormous distinction and a member of a great generation of American biologists. I went also to Madison to be reproached by Dr M. R. Irwin for not having demonstrated that twin cattle on which Bill and I had worked were red-cell chimeras, that is, contained red blood corpuscles of two different genetic origins.

I enjoyed giving my lectures at Harvard and was pleased that they were well received. This was the first of many such sets of lectures I have given in American universities— in Berkeley, for example, Chapel Hill, Dartmouth, and Washington University in Seattle. I have always found it refreshing to lecture before an audience of people who don't already know one's stories and lantern-slides. On arrival in Harvard I found that Maurice Bowra had given some lectures there not long before and had caused some offence by his Oxonian flippancy; he did not take to American victuals and announced his intention of arranging for food parcels to be regularly sent to him from England—an especially unfortunate remark since Bostonians were prominent among those kindly Americans who sent regular consignments of food to England at a time when they were greatly needed. J. B. S. Haldane had also visited Harvard, much to the resentment of such conservative faculty members as Dr Frederick I. Hisaw, who told me he had put Haldane in the social care of Norbert Wiener the mathematician, feeling he had killed two birds with one stone. 'They got on together famously,' Hisaw added with satisfaction. I was not in the least surprised, for their temperaments had much in common and both were extremely brilliant. Dining at the Society of Fellows I had an impressively deep conversation with Willard van Orman Quine on the characteristics one should hope to find in any readable system of logical symbolism, followed by discussion of the degree to which existing systems measured up to these expectations. On the social side I was taken to see a football game (Harvard *v.* Brown) on which I forbear to comment because everything that needs to be said on American football, and much else that need not have been, has been said already.

Like any other green young Englishman, I was also taken to have my nose rubbed in sites of British humiliations in the War of Independence, and in the course of doing so I had a more than adequate opportunity to see and comment on the Fall colours in the forests of New England—of which I need only say the second hundred miles one passes through are very much like what the first were and what the third would prove to be. Although conscious of treading on dangerous ground here, I must add that in my opinion the finest display of Fall colours in the United States is to be seen driving up the Hudson River valley, in the direction of Poughkeepsie.

One way and another I had amassed enough dollars on my American travels to be able to arrange for my wife Jean to stay with me for two weeks in New York City in a comfortable suite in a comfortable second-class hotel just west of Fifth Avenue. Jean took very readily to American breakfasts, especially to those multi-storey pancakes richly interleaved with butter, bacon, and even maple syrup. At each breakfast, thinking of my wallet, I would say with what I hoped was infectious enthusiasm in the American idiom I was beginning to master, 'How about let's go see Grant's tomb?' In real life, however, we usually ended up at Saks Fifth Avenue or walking down Madison Avenue. England was very austere at that time and it was a treat for Jean to look at nylon things, a practice which prompted me to say 'In a few years' time nylon clothing will be strictly for paupers; people with taste and means will buy only the very finest sea island cottons.' It is particularly important that Englishmen in America should wear cotton and not nylon shirts, the reason being that nylon is non-absorbent and the English are not used to environments as warm as are commonplace in

America and are often placed in situations in which they are ill at ease and generally not sure of themselves. In addition to thermal sweating, therefore, they sweat from apocrine glands in the unpleasant way that signifies embarrassment or fear. It is no wonder that the English in America acquired at one time the reputation for being rather smelly, a reputation they kept until they got wise to the use of antiperspirants.

Back in Birmingham I found to my dismay that my colleagues on the Faculty had caused me to become Dean of Science—cruelly onerous work in a provincial university, in which Deans are always traditionally very influential people. The Dean was ex-officio chairman of all committees electing to chairs and of course took the chair at all Faculty meetings, at which he had to have a thorough knowledge and understanding of the business to make sure the Faculty would hold the same opinions as himself. I get no pleasure from the exercise of power, so I regarded being Dean as an intolerable distraction and one which made me specially sympathetic to an offer from University College London, the gist of which was that I should do well to submit my name as a candidate for its Jodrell Chair of Zoology in succession to Professor D. M. S. Watson, shortly retiring. David Meredith Seares Watson was one of the world's foremost vertebrate paleontologists, men of a kind I felt well informed about because I had met Watson's famous peers in America, Alfred Romer and George Gaylord Simpson.

UNIVERSITY COLLEGE
LONDON

The Jodrell Chair was the longest established of all chairs of zoology in England, and University College was the largest and oldest university in the Federation that makes up 'the University of London', so naturally I was tempted to go. Bill promised to join me and we were also accompanied by a very bright and promising recruit, Leslie Brent, who had been President of the Students' Union and was immensely keen to join in the research he knew Bill and I were doing. We moved to London for the term beginning October 1951 where we found the Zoology Department housed in a rambling barn of a building, formerly the warehouse of a famous London store which everybody could remember their mothers having shopped at: Shoolbred's Store in Bloomsbury. When I had asked my old friend Michael Abercrombie, who was already in the College, what the Zoology Department was like, he had said 'I think you should be warned that the entire ground floor is occupied by suites of sumptuous lavatories.' They were not sumptuous but they were numerous, for in accordance with English tradition lavatories had to be differentiated with reference to the prevailing class hierarchy: that is, not only by sex but in effect by the social ranks of staff, students, technicians. The Department also housed a museum that was crying out for demolition and I called to mind Lancelot Hogben, my predecessor in Birmingham, who abolished the museum in his Department there. Indeed, the staff I inherited from Hogben had told me with awe how he had been seen staggering across the campus carrying a stuffed dugong and probably in search of an incinerator. The Prof's distinction of office was to have a private loo that gave on to a fire escape—the whole arrangement being ideally suited to fleeing the premises if I heard noises in the corridor which seemed to portend the arrival of someone I had no wish to see.

Administrative Problems

A professor in a middle-sized English university is a teacher, administrator, probation officer, psychiatrist, and employment agent. He is also a fund-raiser and this last was my most onerous administrative job: although I had no difficulty in raising funds for my own research, it was a very different matter to acquire money for palaeontological research or investigations into the behaviour of spiders. I did my best, though, and amassed about a cubic yard of grant applications, begging letters, thank-you letters, and progress reports. I believed I had established something like a record by having been obliged to apply to nineteen different sources for funds to subsidize the research of a quite small department. My own research was not a problem although it was very much more costly than any other in progress in the Department and it is a pleasure to record most gratefully the help of the Nuffield Foundation and above all of the United States Public Health Service, operating through the National Institutes of Health. Although the United States excels every possible competitor in the proliferation of bureaucratic bullshit as greatly as it excels in many other departments of human activity, I fought my way through it and was rewarded by the handsome funding that kept my little research group solvent during my entire period at University College London—and I am only one among very many European scientists who had reason to be grateful to the United States for the open-handed magnanimity with which they kept so much of European research afloat during our days of penury and shortage after the Second World War. Our Communist sympathizers did their best to depreciate the importance of these acts of grace on the part of the United States and to read discreditable motives into them. At this time, I should add, the activities of the CIA had not yet given reason to think otherwise than warmly about America, so my own attitude towards the

United States has remained that which is proper for a grateful beneficiary.

In London naturally I was invited to serve on a variety of national committees: the most interesting were the Agricultural Research Council (which funded our colleague Leslie Brent to work for his doctor's degree) and the University Grants Committee, the go-between for the Treasury and the universities in the allocation of governmental grants. In spite of one or two naïve administrative aberrations, I believe the Committee did a lot of useful work and promoted the interests of the universities as effectively as it could at a time when it was the duty of the Treasury to keep the purse strings drawn tight. All this committee work was very difficult to sustain because, apart from performing the ordinary duties of a university professor, I was organizing and taking an active part in a time-consuming and onerous research programme, but my experience was that most academic administrators had very little idea of what kind of skills it took to keep all these balls in the air at once.

In my experience, professional administrators have as a rule some kind of sympathy and understanding for research workers, but academics who had 'thrown themselves into administrative life', perhaps because they were academically sterile, had little sympathy for those of us who were trying to administer their departments' work of research and teaching. In my own Department I played fair and did not attempt to delegate to others responsibilities it was my duty to discharge. I was however sometimes obliged mildly to rebuke people who seemed to me to be unduly pressing in their demands for me to procure extra funding for them.

I was proud to have become a member of the Faculty of University College, which was by far the most important of the more recently founded universities and boasted some very distinguished past members. Among them was Ambrose Fleming who had invented the thermionic diode valve, Michael Ventris who deciphered Linear B, and the discoverer of the first recognized 'hormone', *secretin*. This was Ernest A. Starling, a colleague of William Bayliss, one of the foremost physiologists of his day, whose *Principles of General Physiology* can still be read with profit. I also liked the Provost, Ifor Evans, a man with an almost supernatural gift for attracting enormous benefactions into the College coffers—from one donor especially, whose identity has not been officially disclosed to this day. My liking for Ifor Evans made me reflect upon how very lucky I had been with the domestic heads of the institutions in which I had served, especially the two Presidents I had known at Magdalen College: Sir Henry Tizard and the art historian T. S. R. (Tom) Boase who shared my taste in and judgement of opera. Tom had one of the rarest and most enviable conversational gifts—that of correcting people or even contradicting them flatly in a way which so far from snubbing them made them feel all the better for having learnt what they had not known before. Tom learnt how to pronounce the name of the Spanish painter Goya without using the ugly and rather distinctively English *oy* sound as it occurs in toy, boy, or indeed buoy; he taught me also to articulate the sibilant in Degas.

Although I got on very well with Provost Evans, I could not get everything I wanted. Our experimental mice and guinea-pigs were kept at the very top of the building, raising problems of bringing in foodstuffs and removing cage-cleanings and other such trash; I applied therefore to the College Committee for funds to install an elevator in the stairwell. The Chairman of the College Committee, Lord Cohen, did not think much of the proposal and when in a characteristically conscientious way he came in person to discuss what it would entail, he told me, 'When I was at the Ministry during the war none of us thought anything of walking up four or five flights of stairs.' 'But,' I said, 'I expect none of you was carrying a sack full of rabbit faeces at the time.' He took the point and in due course I was allowed to fit a hoist into the stairwell. This served the purpose admirably.

University College had a cosy, friendly atmosphere and it was easy to begin to develop feelings of loyalty towards it—though not, I fear, towards the University of London, the administrative structure and procedures of which were designed to create and perpetuate the illusion that it was a single integral university with a number of constituent colleges subordinate to it, such as University College, King's College, and Imperial College. The fostering of this illusion meant that a tier of University committees was superimposed upon the College Committee and matters had to be arranged so that functions best performed by the Colleges, such as appointments to chairs, should be so conducted as to make it appear that these were University, not College, appointments. The duplication of business which the University illusion necessitated made the University of London the most tiresome academic institution in the Western world—and in some ways, I felt, the most inefficient.

My Zoology Department was a rambling gormenghastly structure with many rooms in unexpected places and I was happy to be able to put my predecessor, Professor D. M. S. Watson, into a suite of rooms where he could continue working on his fossils with a secretary and assistant.

The teaching staff I inherited at University College were a quite exceptionally intelligent and likeable lot, enriched by a number of visiting workers with unusual capability: from the United Kingdom, Alex Comfort, the biochemist, poet, and novelist; Anne McLaren, who became one of the few women Fellows of the Royal Society; Donald Michie, now England's foremost authority on 'machine intelligence'; and a number of American guests—Paul Terasaki, Paul Russell, Jerry Lawrence, and Bill Hildeman. In addition the Department of Biometry, of which J. B. S. Haldane was the head, was physically housed in my Department, though not administratively a part of it, thank God.

The American guests were friendly and well liked and wonderfully patient with the teasing they had to put up with from the department, the worst offender being Haldane whose favourite provocation was to argue that civil liberties were every bit as much endangered in the USA as in Russia and East Europe. One of my American guests one December came to complain to me formally that there was no daytime in England: night fell with commendable regularity but he got up in the dark and night fell, it seemed to him, almost immediately after. I couldn't help sympathizing with him because University College was surrounded by the principal main-line railway stations at a time when steam trains were still darkening the sky with soot and grime.

This company, at least two of whom were notable conversationalists, made our tea-table the liveliest and the wittiest I have ever attended, but we trod very warily when we came to politics: Haldane was a card-carrying Party member who was a frequent contributor to the *Daily Worker*, on which he had served as chairman of the editorial board. He was a complete innocent politically and believed everything he was told. I can remember asking him if he did not think it very strange that the lately disgraced Beria, in spite of the exalted position he held in the state, had all the while been in the pay of the Americans. Haldane was not in the least surprised. 'People in high-up positions sometimes get careless, you know.' Haldane also heartily approved of the murder in Czechoslovakia of the politicians Clementis and Slansky.

Haldane worked in a room which was never tidied or cleaned. The fossils upon which he was proposing one day to undertake some biometric studies were clearly undergoing a second interment, the sediments consisting this time of atmospheric dust and soot, together with manuscripts, committee papers, and official communications of the College. When anything got lost, Haldane always claimed it was something of *their* doing. His liking and admiration for the working classes was purely notional and his colleagues soon formed the opinion that he couldn't bear the sight of them; it was the laugh of the Department when electricians whose duty it was to rewire his office demanded danger money for working in it. Haldane's paranoia was sometimes an embarrassment. I can remember his agreeing to take the chair at a public University lecture given by a famous American zoologist and geneticist. He excused himself at the last moment saying that his performing the function would be too embarrassing to the lecturer because he (Haldane) had once reacted 'rather violently' when he had been the victim of a sexual assault by the lecturer's wife. This lady was a comfortable middle-aged body who, I should say from my knowledge of American manners, probably once slipped her arm through his and said 'Come on Jack, let's go in to supper.' Odd though this may seem, this may have been enough to offend Haldane, who was all crazy—mixed-up on matters of sex. Ronald Clark in his definitive biography of Haldane* refers to his 'bawdiness and boasting of his sexual prowess'. I created no opportunity to make myself aware of this side of his character. Julian Huxley, for whom Haldane once fagged† at Eton, told me that he was not physically equipped to perform sexually, a circumstance that did nothing to impair his mind, the best in University College.

Haldane's having been chairman of the editorial board of the *Daily Worker*, combined with the strongly Communist sympathies of several members of the staff, made the Zoology Department of the College, and perhaps even the College as a whole, an object of suspicion by Intelligence. When the time came for me to receive a modest civil honour—to become a Commander of the British Empire—as a reward for my administrative services to the Agricultural Research Council, I had a long interview with a civil but, as I thought, rather silly Intelligence Officer who did not disclose the name of the agency for which he was working; he was determined to find out if I was at heart one of those intolerant and hot-headed people who felt that nothing could meliorate the lot of the working classes other than a revolution that would cause the blood of the aristocracy to flow down the gutters of Park Lane. He wondered, for example, why I did not terminate the employment of the left-wing members of my Department and why they had been to Czechoslovakia. I explained the facts about University

---

* *J. B. S. The Life and Work of J. B. S. Haldane* (London, 1968; Oxford, 1984).

† A fag is a boy who acts as a servant to an older boy—a procedure alleged to be good for the character of the younger one.

appointments and that professors were not the employers of their staff. I think I gave him a first insight into the international character of science. The chap was satisfied with my answers and sent me a cheery letter of congratulation when in due course he read in the papers that I had taken up command of the British Empire.

At University College I had another hugely risible encounter with Intelligence. I had accepted a short-term consultancy to a committee chaired by Lord Todd to inquire into a number of technical and administrative matters to do with chemical warfare, work that would entail my receiving a number of secret, perhaps Top Secret, documents. On this occasion another chap came to see me and elucidated the principles of security: he explained that documents should on no account be thrown into waste-paper baskets or their contents made the subject of lively conversation in the bar of the Marlborough Arms, a nearby public house and the Department's favourite committee room. No one should have an inkling that I was engaged on secret work, least of all the many Communist sympathizers in the Department. I kept my side of the bargain and can vouch that no one thought of me as a repository of secrets, although they did not keep their side of the bargain anything like so well. When I was to receive a Top Secret document, a private soldier arrived outside the Zoology Department on a sputtering and explosive motor-bike that he brought to rest immediately outside the lecture room. Like the frog footman in *Alice* he was carrying an important-looking missive and he insisted on putting it directly into my hands, so instantly cancelling all my own tactful reticence. There is nothing about the British record on matters of security to make me think this comic travesty was unusual.

Cricket

One of the most agreeable aspects of life in University College was the opportunity it offered to play village cricket. The graduate student we had brought with us from Birmingham, Leslie Brent, represented our closest approximation to a sportsman, for he had played hockey for the Combined English Universities and now turned his attention to organizing cricket. From staff of both sexes, graduate students, and guest workers—especially Americans, who took naturally to the game—we assembled a team of eleven players willing to challenge teams from other Departments, and even villages and small colleges. The game gave one opportunity to spend at least an afternoon in the open air and usually in very pleasant surroundings, enjoying the prospect or retrospect of lunch or tea accompanied by a pint of ale. One cannot stand alone in an open field without inviting public comment, but it's all right when twenty-one others are doing so too. We had a number of traditional rivals such as the Botany Department, whom we usually made short work of. The Radiobiology Research Unit at Harwell were more of a match for us, although unfortunately Harwell (housing the laboratory of the UK Atomic Energy Authority) was not designed with an eye to cricket, so the ground was not of the kind that encouraged the players to gulp in draughts of fresh air as they trotted onto the field. We played in fact on a matting wicket fairly laid out upon what looked like a radiation-blasted terrain.

I continued the health-giving practice of the occasional game of cricket when I became Director of the National Institute for Medical Research at Mill Hill a few years later. The game I remember most vividly was one I had hurried back from a conference in Paris to play in after a late and splendid farewell party of the International Congress of the Transplantation Society. Being a very large research institute the National Institute for Medical Research could field a stronger team than our little Zoology Department and was more ambitious in challenging opponents. This game was a match against a London College team, one member of which was a young and aggressive fast bowler, not used to having his bowling hit punitively around. I played for the NIMR team in my capacity as an 'all rounder'—a technical term in village cricket referring to someone equally lacking in proficiency in all branches of the game.

Research at University College

Now began the most fruitful period of my academic life: Bill, Leslie Brent, and I knew exactly what we wanted to do and had no serious misgivings about our ability to do it. Our ambition was to bring about by design the immunological phenomenon that occurs naturally in twin cattle, namely to reduce, even abolish, their power to recognize and destroy genetically foreign tissues. We hoped to do this by inoculating embryos with 'foreign' living cells, all of the same genetic provenance, before the embryos' immunological faculties had matured. Working with genetically homogeneous, inbred strains of mice we began by ascertaining as precisely as we could how long such a skin graft would survive when transplanted from one animal to another. This was dull spadework, but it had to be done before we could evaluate how successful were our efforts in diminishing or abolishing the resistance of one strain of mice to the transplantation of skin grafts from another. The unborn or foetal mice, in which we hoped to induce a state of immunological 'tolerance', were inoculated through the body wall of their mother—an extraordinarily simple operation that did not usually interfere with gestation. This made possible the test of our hypothesis: that a brown mouse of strain CBA, which had before birth received an inoculation of living cells from white mice of a strain A, would, when adult, accept a skin graft from mice of strain A. Normally this graft would be rejected, with the accompaniment of a violent inflammatory reaction 10–12 days after transplantation.

For one reason or another some of the experiments failed, but it was not very long—considering how many things might have gone wrong—before we had established that an inoculated CBA mouse could accept an A strain skin-graft which survived. Survival times varied, of course, however much one tried to standardize the conditions under which transplantations were carried out, but the survival time we now encountered was something that would occur by mere luck only once in several thousand trials.

We felt, therefore, that we were on to a genuine phenomenon to which, by analogy with 'acquired immunity', we gave the name 'acquired immunological tolerance', for we had artificially reproduced the mutual tolerance we had observed in twin cattle. Quite independently of cattle, similar examples of tolerance had, we now realized, been described many times before by embryologists. They had often grafted organ rudiments from one embryo into another and watched them being incorporated into the alien recipient, just as easily as if they had developed naturally. In the meantime, Milan Hašek, a very gifted Czechoslovak biologist, arranged a vascular union—a parabiosis—between two chicken embryos, thus reproducing the state of affairs that occurred in the cattle twins. He found that the chickens hatched from these parabionts were now tolerant of each other's red blood corpuscles; had they not been put in vascular union the egg would have rejected them. We repeated Hašek's work and confirmed his results. Such simultaneous discoveries are not uncommon in science, but what was remarkable was that Hašek's motivation was entirely different from our own. He was a Communist Party member who had been taken in by the metaphysics and nature-philosophy of Michurin and Lysenko that repudiated Mendelian genetics, and with his experiment hoped to repudiate Mendelian genetics. There could not be a better example of how false premises, metaphysical fancies even, may lead to empirically sound conclusions, a circumstance that reinforces Popper's warning against the vulgar error of dismissing all metaphysical speculation as so much gobbledegook.

The three of us announced our findings at a conference in 1944 organized by the Ciba Foundation on the Preservation and Transplantation of Tissues, but it was not until 1953 that we published the discovery in a short article in *Nature*, so reaching a world-wide audience. The real significance of the discovery of immunological tolerance was to show that the problem of transplanting tissues from one individual to another was soluble, even though the experimental methods we had developed in the laboratory could not be applied to human beings. What had been established for the first time was the possibility of breaking down the natural barrier that prohibits the transplantation of genetically foreign tissues: some people had maintained that this was in principle impossible, since substances that provoke the normal rejection reaction are part of the genetic make-up, something that could no more be changed than one's blood group. In addition, in evolutionary terms, the rejection of genetically foreign grafts has a history of more than a hundred million years, being already present in force at the time bony fish evolved. There were good reasons, then, for people to believe that the human transplantation problem was insoluble, in so far as it entailed using tissues or organs from voluntary donors. Our experimental findings did away once and for all with what Winston Churchill described as 'Theshe dark counshels'.

Thus the ultimate importance of the discovery of tolerance turned out to be not practical, but moral. It put new heart into the many biologists and surgeons who were working to make it possible to graft, for example, kidneys from one person to another—a procedure already shown to be both genetically and physiologically possible by the brilliantly successful transplantation of a kidney from a patient's identical twin donor, at the Peter Brent Brigham Hospital in Boston. This was an exceptionally fertile period for those of us working on transplantation biology, and shortly afterwards, another important advance was made by Billingham and Brent, to the accompaniment of encouraging noises from the touch-line from myself. They discovered an altogether new aspect of the immunological response. Usually a graft is recognized as foreign by the host—the animal into which it is transplanted— and is soon cast off by an immunological response. But when the graft consists of, or contains, cells such as lymphocytes, which are capable of mounting an immunological response, something quite different happens. When lymphocytes are in the graft, and when the host is, or has been made, tolerant of the graft, the tables are turned. Now the graft attacks the host and causes a wasting disease—'graft versus host' (GvH) disease or 'runt disease', as Bill named it.

There were some interesting methodological parallels, or coincidences, between the discoveries of tolerance and graft versus host disease. Just as our discovery of tolerance had been paralleled by the discoveries made by Milan Hašek working in Prague, so the discovery of GvH disease was matched by the simultaneous discovery of an example of it by Dr Morten Simonsen working in Copenhagen. Indeed, this whole period was a golden age of immunology, an age abounding in important synthetic discoveries* all over the world, a time when we all thought it good to be alive. We who were working on these problems all knew each other, and met as often as we could to exchange ideas and hot news from the laboratory.

I hope no one will conclude that our research programme at University College was one long march of triumph; no real-life research is ever so, and we had a number of setbacks of which the most serious was over establishing the chemical identity of the immunity-provoking substances that arouse resistance to transplanted grafts. Whereas the discovery of tolerance was the outcome of collaborative work to which all three of us contributed, I must claim the lion's share of the discredit for forming a quite mistaken opinion about the chemical nature of these antigens: a series of injudiciously interpreted experiments combined, I think, with one or two technical shortcomings, led me to form the erroneous opinion that transplantation antigens were deoxyribonucleoproteins. This would have been an extremely important hypothesis had later work corroborated it, but it did not. The real mischief done by such mistakes is to waste time and this one was a real

---

* An *analytic discovery* is a mapping of territory already known to exist—for example, the elucidation of the crystalline structure of a molecular species which is known a priori to have a crystalline structure. By contrast, *synthetic discovery* is an entering upon territory not until then known to exist. Immunological tolerance was a synthetic discovery, so was GvH disease, and so was Dr James Gowans's discovery that lymphocytes were circulating cells as red blood corpuscles are. Another example would be the discovery by Jacques Miller and Robert A. Good that the thymus gland is crucially important for the maturing and development of those lymphocytes responsible for the transaction of many immunological reactions.

time-waster—a material injury much more serious in the long term than the loss of face involved in being the champion of a mistaken view.

Sometime in the summer of 1960 the then administrative head of the Medical Research Council, Sir Harold Himsworth, invited me to lunch at his club, abetting his advocacy by that well known to be exercised by Château Cheval Blanc. He put it to me that when the then incumbent Sir Charles Harington retired in 1962, I should take over the Directorship of the National Institute for Medical Research at Mill Hill. The proposal did not make an immediate appeal because I was very contented at University College, where my research was prospering and I got some pleasure from teaching the students. I already knew Mill Hill as an enormous scientific barracks which, having no students, would not be meliorated by the patter of tiny feet. Moreover, although I was confident of my competence in the area of experimental pathology, I was well aware of how unsuited I was to direct research of a predominantly chemical or biochemical character, such as much of the research then in progress at Mill Hill. But in spite of these protests I said I would give the proposal very serious consideration, having at the same time the frightened foreboding that I should accept. My friend John Humphrey whom I, in common with many others, regarded as the leading immunologist in England, was working at Mill Hill and he told me enough about the way it worked to make me feel confident I could handle the job. The most important single consideration was that Mill Hill had only one master, the Medical Research Council: so I should not be engaged in the endless writing of begging and thank-you letters which went with being a university prof. In the event, I agreed to take over the job from 1 August 1962—but some exciting events were to occur in the mean time.

One October evening in 1960, when I got home from work, I had a phone call from a journalist in Stockholm who wanted to know if I was a friend of Sir Macfarlane Burnet. I told him of our relationship, but had no idea and did not enquire why he had asked. But the next morning I read in *The Times* that

Burnet and I were to share the 1960 Nobel Prize for 'Medicine or Physiology', the citation being 'for the discovery of acquired immunological tolerance'. I was terribly sorry that the distinction could not be so far subdivided as to have included my friends Bill and Leslie. I could, of course—and did—share my portion of the prize money with them, but that's not the same thing. I did not work for the distinction, did not expect to get it, and did not know who my nominators were, though I made what I believe to have been accurate guesses. It is in keeping with the general disproportion of the importance attached to the Nobel Prize among laymen that the effect of an award upon a small academic institution is almost seismic in character. Certainly the telephone switchboard of University College was pretty well put out of commission for the day, for reasons that the telephonists did not clearly understand.

Laureate's Mailbag etc.

Immediately upon his designation as such, a Nobel Laureate becomes beneficiary—or, as most of them believe, the victim—of a variant of the kind of notoriety enjoyed by pop stars and anyone reputed by the media to be a 'personality'. Overnight a Laureate is deemed to have become an authority on all the problems that plague society. His opinion is sought upon the efficacy and propriety of fertilizing human ova inside the body, on the desirability of nuclear weapons, the fitness of women for holy orders, and much else besides. The contents of his mailbag change accordingly, for in addition to the professional man's usual ration of letters from persons offering to make his fortune, there are letters from people suggesting various means by which he may make theirs. One favourite proposal is to ask the Laureate to 'enter on the attached form' answers to an enclosed sheet which contains questions such as 'Do you believe in God?' or, 'Do you believe, if there is no personal God, that God is represented by a diffuse benevolence that somehow pervades the entire universe?' A Laureate foolish enough to answer this questionnaire may find that in a month's time he features prominently in a book entitled *Does God Exist?—The Scientist Speaks*. Over and above this there are innumerable requests for autographs, signed cabinet-size photographs, pages of manuscript, personal letters wishing the applicant good cheer and good fortune, all to be answered in the Laureate's own hand. Autograph signatures, it may be explained, have a certain monetary value—as with all other things thought worth collecting, they are valued inversely to their degree of abundance. I only sign autographs when they are accompanied by a self-addressed envelope; I rather suspect that Francis Crick signs none, and that *his* autographs are accordingly worth ten or twenty Medawars. The more obliging Laureates doubtless sign everything and don't realize that they are undermining their market value. Of greater importance, perhaps, are the manifestos and declarations that the Laureate is asked to give his authority to. If these are temperately worded pleas intended to persuade foreign despots to abstain from persecuting their fellow-men, well and good, but more often Laureates are asked to sign uncontroversial manifestos such as that which I quote in my book *Advice to a Young Scientist*: The nations of the world must henceforward live together in amity and concord and abjure the use of warfare as a means of settling political disputes.

A Laureate really desperate for time to get on with research or other proper business may well have recourse to a checklist such as that used by Francis Crick to cope with importunities.* Crick cannot reasonably be accused of

---

* I quote from Harriet Zuckerman's *Scientific Élite* (New York, 1977): 'Dr Crick thanks you for your letter but regrets that he is unable to accept your kind invitation to:

send an autograph	help you in your project
provide a photograph	read your manuscript
cure your disease	deliver a lecture
be interviewed	attend a conference
talk on the radio	act as chairman
appear on TV	become an editor
speak after dinner	write a book
give a testimonial	accept an honorary degree.'

arrogance or callousness for using this checklist, because he devoted the time thus saved to research in collaboration with Dr Sidney Brenner which elucidated the nucleotide alphabet of the genetic code—work in my opinion worthy of a second Nobel Prize.

two s, *two* d

'Do you have children?' I was asked by the very distinguished Professor of Theoretical Physics shortly after I joined the staff of Birmingham University. 'Four,' I replied, 'equally spaced and alternating in sex'; and because my interlocutor was a theoretical physicist known to be privy to the dark secrets of the atomic bomb, I added 'We biologists do not choose that a number of facts about reproduction should become generally known.' The physicist did not realize I was teasing, and for a moment I think he was rattled by the implication that a mere biologist might know something that a theoretical physicist did not.

I had thought, when I was a boy, that I should be a good father, one who wisely and kindly guided my children, shaping their minds and morals by imperceptible degrees. My performance fell so far short of these ambitions that I was an outstandingly rotten father and neglected my children disgracefully. I was not a bad father in the sense of shouting at and browbeating them and certainly never hitting them, even in anger—which Bernard Shaw rightly described as the only excusable reason for doing so. My neglect was due to my total preoccupation with research in the laboratory, writing, or delivering one or other of the very many lectures I was repeatedly asked for. These included the BBC's Reith Lectures which I prepared in the summer of 1959 for delivery in the autumn; this was the most time-consuming commission I ever undertook, because it involved reading and mastering all the papers of the Royal Commission on Population and all the official demographic records that are published from the office of the Registrar-General. During most of this August my family were away on a sailing holiday in Cornwall—something I could not very easily join in, being no sailor. I worked in my office in University College every night for a long period, and because one acquires a momentum that is difficult to halt I tended to stay on every night until 2 or 3.00 a.m. By so doing I brought a little colour and variety into the otherwise drab and humdrum lives of the night watchmen who found the entire proceeding inexplicable. I am ashamed to say that I smoked cigarettes heavily during the whole of this period of preparation, thus no doubt making me perilously vulnerable to the frightful illness that struck me down a few years later.

In general, I took a lot of exercise in the manner characteristic of obsessionals—that is to say in the form of short periods of intense and doubtless health-endangering activity on the squash or tennis court, supplemented by early-morning swimming in company with two *s* in the rather splendid swimming pool of the London borough in which I live. The only sane form of exercise indulged in was weekend village cricket on Saturdays and Sundays, which I have already mentioned. With hindsight I can see that during all this time I had severe hypertension, the discomfort of which was greatly relieved by violent exercise which made me feel I was catching up with my heart. When I became Director of the NIMR my colleague Eugene Lance and I made a point of running up six flights of stairs to the Institute's restaurant and on reaching the top whistling a patriotic song to demonstrate to each other our fitness to do so.

I mentioned writing as one of my activities, something that came to play a more and more important part in my creative life. My books started as collections of essays, extended book reviews, transcripts of lectures, and other occasional pieces. My publishers were a bit sniffy about them ('When are you going to write a *proper* book?'). The first, *The Uniqueness of the Individual*, appeared in 1957 (Dover Publications produced a second revised edition in 1981). I still think it gave a true picture of what young biologists were thinking about before the Enlightenment ushered in by the recognition of DNA as the vector of genetic information. This first collection is full of ideas and contains the only full account of my neo-Darwinian theory of the evolution of an ageing process and a first outline of what I was later to call exogenetic evolution. It even hints at the notion of 'kin selection', which plays such an important part today in sociobiological thought. It also contains an essay, 'The Uniqueness of the Individual', which gave the book its title and which attracted a number of bright medical students into the surgery of transplantation.

The second collection of essays, *The Art of the Soluble*, did not appear until 1967: it contained a number of lectures, and a piece on D'Arcy Wentworth Thompson who held a University chair first at Dundee and then at St Andrews for a total of sixty-four years, that is, for the length of time most of us are allowed between birth to retirement from professional employment. It also contained a review of Teilhard de Chardin's *The Phenomenon of Man*, written at the special request of my old friend and colleague Gilbert Ryle, the editor of the philosophic journal *Mind*, because he was at his wits' end to know whom to entrust the book to. Preparing this review was my first literary task when I arrived at University College. I thought it extremely funny and laughed a lot when in quoting one of Teilhard's more portentous passages I was able to write after it '[my Romans]'. As I hammered the piece out on the little portable typewriter in my office my laughter could be heard all the way down the corridor. A number of psychologists tried to 'interpret' my review. The idea that it was a piece of literary criticism did not enter their heads—one at least preferred to see it as an Oedipal slaying of my heavenly Father. I am one of those who feels quite strongly that writing, however solemn or formal, should sound like speech—and for this reason I soon gave up bashing away on my typewriter and took to the Dictaphone, an action made possible by my singular good fortune in having had a succession of highly intelligent secretaries.

In the main these earlier books received appreciative reviews, and they remained so until I achieved a degree of proficiency in writing that attracted the animosity and therefore the snide kind of response from literary intellectuals.

But I am wandering off the subject of two *s*, two *d*; my digression on writing is mainly excusatory and part of the case for the defence of a bad father. I observed wonderingly of my children, as many parents have observed of theirs, how early in life certain apparently deep-seated traits of character are established and how little they change as children grow up. I am thinking of traits such as providence, compassion, and equanimity.

I am very happy to be able to say that my many and grievous shortcomings as a parent apparently did no lasting damage to my children. There can be no 'control' for such a statement but at least I avoided being parental to a fault, that is, altogether too intrusive and bossy and too anxious to create my children in my own image. None of the children became a professional scientist and I exerted no pressure to make them so. I am quite certain, though, that all four of them were intelligent, imaginative, and energetic enough to have become good scientists, though I am glad they did not: one obsessional in the family is enough. All four may have imbibed by the kind of osmosis that works in families their father's single-mindedness in their address to what they do, and I am pleased with and proud of their eventual choice of careers: psychologist, investigative journalist, businesswoman, and professional yachtsman—who sailed the Atlantic single-handed in a boat far too small for the purpose—an admirable mix from the standpoint of family life.

One *s* and two *d* made unwise first marriages and have tried again with great success. There are five natural grandchildren, the tally increasing to eight if step-grandchildren are counted in, as of course they are. All are as bright and as different from each other as human beings can be. As an afterthought I dedicate this book to them too, because one day I think it will amuse them to know something about their wicked great-uncle Philip.

I do remember one disinterested effort that I made on the children's behalf: on Sunday mornings I played gramophone records through an enormous HMV horn, conducting them where I thought appropriate—now for 'Fate knocking on the door' and so on. I enjoyed these concerts too, for being able to hear again some of the most familiar music through others' ears, especially the ears of children, revives and refreshes its original appeal for oneself, so that I was once again carried away by Tchaikovsky's First Piano Concerto and Beethoven's 'Moonlight' Sonata.

The fact that the children grew up into busy, mature adults coping with family responsibilities more successfully, I believe, than I did, will not deceive any experienced reader into thinking that they did not pass through some very difficult periods in the course of growing-up. These were quite a trial to Jean and myself. I report accordingly a fragment of dialogue that throws some light on Jean's character and on the relationship between us. After one *d* had been more than usually tiresome, I said to Jean 'How much longer have we got to be patient, forbearing, loving and understanding?' 'The rest of our lives, or for as long as she needs it,' Jean replied. It was a lesson in the nature of parental responsibility that I never forgot.

THE NATIONAL INSTITUTE FOR
MEDICAL RESEARCH

North London blends imperceptibly with the beautiful countryside of south Middlesex and just at the point at which a real doubt arises about which is which, town or country, there stands the National Institute for Medical Research. In accordance with the way these things go in the Government service, the Director of the Institute, Sir Charles Harington, D.Sc.* was fully engaged in his onerous and responsible employment on 31 July 1962, whereas on 1 August 1962 he was out of work and I was Director. The Institute is the largest medical research organization in the British Commonwealth; several hundred scientists are grouped together into Divisions each headed by someone having duties somewhat akin to those of a university professor. The administration of such an Institute is a hell of a job and it had occupied the whole of Sir Charles Harington's time. I was amazingly lucky that I succeeded such a superb administrator. During the war the NIMR had been taken over by the Admiralty and designated a training 'ship' of the Royal Navy. The naval parallel gained added strength from the circumstance that the Institute rode high on one of the wolds which, alternating with valleys, make up the characteristic landscape of south Middlesex. My good fortune in succeeding Harington grew out of the fact that he ran the Institute like a Royal Naval ship's captain: he knew everybody and every inch of the building, each crack in the plaster, each shortcoming in the pointing of the bricks, and each instance of dampness where all should have been dry. He knew every member of staff and, moreover, read and

* I mention this degree to emphasize that Harington was not medically qualified, a shortcoming that led to a question being asked about him in the House of Commons. I myself, as I have explained, was not even a D.Phil.—but this the legislature fortunately overlooked.

commented on every paper they wrote. In this work he had been helped for very many years by a woman of a kind much more common in America than in the United Kingdom: in America she has some such title as 'Assistant to the President', knows all the staff of the organization she serves, and has such a complete grasp of its business that, in all but name, she is the tactical boss and runs the place from day to day—in my experience very successfully indeed.

Pauline Townend, whom I inherited as my secretary, was a woman of this calibre; the circumstance of inheriting her and enjoying Harington's administrative arrangements made my taking over the Directorship a change of occupation no more strenuous than that of sliding over into the driving-seat of a Rolls-Royce.

I devoted my first few weeks as Director to pastoral duties—visiting the whole Institute, meeting and trying to memorize the names of every member of the staff, some of whom were fairly humdrum journeyman scientists, others very good, and just a few outstandingly brilliant. Some four or five were depressives. I could cope with them only by pretending to be a depressive myself and discussing with them at length what was best for our situation ('I *never* take tranquillizers: do you?' and 'I drink very little: it doesn't improve things a bit') and at the end of such a sermon my lay patient was much improved, though I was depressed by the thought that the whole exercise would have to be repeated as often as it was necessary. The most gifted of the depressives, Alick Isaacs, alternated his depressive moods with hypo-manic bouts which were much more difficult to cope with; in his hypomania, ideas poured out of him. They were fruitful or unsound in about the proportion one would have expected, but they came abnormally fast.

Certainly the general level of proficiency made me very proud that I had become Director of the Institute. I know that many people assumed that I should not be able to continue with my research while being Director, but administrative duties do nothing to still what Immanuel Kant had described as the 'restless endeavour' to make sense of things, which is a true scientist's most reliable distinguishing mark. Being a quick worker I found that if I spent the first hour or two of the day reading and answering letters, I was then free for the rest of the day to carry on with research at the bench, joining my old friend Leslie Brent in an upstairs laboratory one floor up (Rupert Billingham had already left to take an appointment of professorial rank in the United States, ending as a departmental head in the Medical School in Dallas, Texas). I hardly ever used the telephone myself and disliked being telephoned. If one writes, one has a record of what is said: constant use of the telephone is a mark of a bad administrator. The administration was not markedly more onerous than it had been at University College and I soon reaped the benefits of having only one financial master. I felt indeed rather as the actress Mrs Patrick Campbell, who compared marriage to the exchange of 'the hurlyburly of the *chaise longue* for the deep, deep peace of the double bed'.

Research prospered, though Leslie Brent and I made no further discovery of the same stature as that of immunological tolerance. We addressed ourselves to the problem of how in principle we could choose the most highly compatible transplant donor for a given recipient when there was a panel of donors to choose from. By following up a chance observation, we made the interesting though minor discovery that if normal lymphocytes derived from one guinea-pig or human being were to be injected into the skin of another guinea-pig or human being they would raise a local reaction accompanied by the so-called 'delayed' type of inflammatory response—that which contrasts with the dramatic weal-and-flare response characteristic of the immediate type of hyper-sensitivity. The skin reaction excited by the intradermal injection of normal lymphocytes did not begin until about five hours after the injection—the 'first inflammatory episode' —and then became progressively more pronounced (the 'flare-up') until it quite quickly subsided and faded away. We had no difficulty at all in showing that this was a manifestation of the 'graft-versus-host' reaction that Bill and Leslie had discovered a few years beforehand; that is to say, it was an immunological reaction mounted by the injected lymphocytes against the animal into which they had been injected. It was a graft rejection reaction in reverse and it offered us a way into the deeper analysis of the rejection process. We interpreted the first inflammatory episode as the only immunological element in the whole reaction, the only recognition of and reaction against non-self. The 'flare-up' we interpreted as a reproduction on the tiny scale on which we were working of the 'proliferative' episode of a normal immune response— that which amplifies the reaction from a merely local phenomenon to something that might come into force over the whole body. We were also greatly surprised to find* that conventional immunosuppressive agents and procedures such as X-irradiation had almost no effect on the first inflammatory episode but diminished, and at suitable doses completely abolished, the flare-up. From this we drew the far-reaching conclusion that immunosuppressive agents, so called, are not really suppressive agents at all: they interfere only with the amplification of the immune response and therefore its expression at a systemic level as opposed to a merely local level. A number of quantitative studies using different numbers of cells to elicit our so-called 'normal lymphocyte transfer reaction' led us to form the opinion that the intensity of an immunological reaction did not express the reactivity of an individual lymphocyte but was rather an expression of the *number* of lymphocytes engaged in the response: each lymphocyte either did or did not perform immunologically. We satisfied ourselves by experiments using guinea-pigs that the reaction we were studying *could* certainly be used for the selection of donors, as we had hoped when we began, but the procedure did not come into clinical use because improvement in immunosuppressive procedures and in the availability of other methods of selection of donors rendered our much more elaborate scheme of selection unnecessary.

* L. Brent and P. B. Medawar, 'Quantitative studies on tissue transplantation immunity. VII. The normal lymphocyte transfer reaction', *Proceedings of the Royal Society Bulletin*, clxv (1966, 281–307; 'Cellular immunity and the homograft reaction', *British Medical Bulletin*, xxiii (1967), 55–9.

I believe that my deep involvement in research at the bench, with its clear implication of the overriding importance I attached to it, set a good example in the Institute, because it was also clear at the same time that I was not skimping the most important part of my administrative task which was, of course, to look after and generally to promote the welfare of members of the staff. The Director's other main function was to negotiate with the Medical Research Council for funds to purchase the necessary research apparatus and to enable members of staff to travel to the conferences and get-togethers all over the world which are one of the most attractive features of the scientific life. These procedures were not very difficult or time-consuming: they required only concentrated attention and quick decision-making, and with the expert secretarial help that I got they could easily be streamlined.

The general atmosphere of the Institute was very good and all our many visiting workers, especially Americans, remarked it. Because of the high degree of job security, the decent length of contracts of employment that the Council offered, and above all the fact that scientific staff had no reason to feel that research opportunities were denied them through lack of funds or facilities, there was less competitiveness in the Institute than in any other comparable organization I have known, and accordingly less intriguing for self-advancement than can be found elsewhere. I saw it as my principal duty to create and sustain an environment conducive to the advancement of learning and to make recommendations to the MRC for funding of the areas of biomedical research most urgently in need. My function was *not* what one Minister of Science supposed it to be, that of issuing orders from my desk about the research in which each member of the staff would be engaged. I told the Minister when he visited the Institute that if my function had been that of a petty academic dictator, then all the people in the Institute whose services the MRC was most anxious to retain would promptly seek employment elsewhere. Many research workers *did* seek employment elsewhere in the ordinary course of things, but as a former

Director of the Institute, Sir Henry Dale, had said, he would rather the NIMR were a nursery for future professors than an asylum for research workers who had failed to secure academic advancement.

I was pursuing my career with unobtrusive lunacy, conducting the administration of the Institute, and researching with Dr Ray Levey and subsequently with a brilliant young orthopaedic surgeon, Eugene Lance, upon the characteristics of a new and, as it seemed to us, very promising immunosuppressive agent, antithymocyte serum.

Throughout the year I played violent games of squash and I smoked—particularly 5-cent American cigars, bought in packs of 500 from a local newsagent on my way in to work. (I had of course given up cigarette-smoking on my appointment to the Directorship, reflecting that although the director of a medical research institute might get away with rape, murder, battery or arson, smoking cigarettes was definitely out.) I accepted many lectureships and thought nothing of visiting the USA for a day or two and returning overnight so as to be back at my desk by 8.30 a.m. In one bad period I was visiting the States about once a month. It was on one of these visits— to attend a meeting on transplantation organized by the New York Academy of Sciences—that I fell in with Eugene Lance, who expressed a wish to come to spend a post-doctoral year working in collaboration with me. We discussed the matter in the Faculty Club of Rockefeller University, drinking more than enough Gibsons* to form a lasting friendship. After my serious illness, Eugene pretty well kept me going as a creative scientist by staying on in our laboratory until I could stand on my own feet again.

This kind of transatlantic commuting is no way to go on because apart from endangering health, it is a proceeding that

---

* A Gibson is not much different from neat gin containing a pearl onion. The Rockefeller Faculty Club, where reputations are most critically appraised, contains the best graffito known to me: a *New Yorker* cartoon showing three earnest scholars of the Stone Age discussing Prometheus. 'Sure he discovered fire,' one of them is saying, 'but what has he done since?'

makes one rather inhuman, selfishly guarding every second of one's time and becoming inattentive about personal relationships: one soon formed the opinion that anyone who used three words where two would have done was a bore of insufferable prolixity whose company must at all costs be shunned. A danger sign that fellow-obsessionals will at once recognize is the tendency to regard the happiest moments of your life as those that occur when someone who has an appointment to see you is prevented from coming.

This way of life no doubt contributed to my continuing a gold medallist for bad parenthood. It couldn't go on; and it didn't.

It did not take me many weeks to make up my mind about the shortcomings of the Institute and the steps that might be taken to remedy them. I had thought it anomalous, for example, that one of the world's principal centres of experimental biology should lack a department of genetics and of developmental biology. Moreover, having been built as a kind of scientific barracks, there was no place in the Institute where scientific workers might sit over a glass of ale and discuss their ideas for experiments with colleagues and friends. Nothing served the Institute as the Marlborough Arms served University College or the Lamb and Flag served the Oxford science laboratories. Before I left we had a place to sit and a modest bar along which to converse.

The housing and husbandry of the Institute's colonies of mice and guinea-pigs had at one time been the best in the country and a model that other institutions strove to copy. Now they were sadly out of date: experiments in progress had too often been spoiled by the deaths of experimental subjects through intercurrent infections, resulting in the need to breed an unnecessarily large number of animals. We decided that the NIMR should again provide a model for the experimental welfare of animals. The colonies were refounded on a 'SPF' basis in which breeding mice, delivered by Caesarean section, were reared under the strictest conditions of hygiene and freedom from infection. ('SPF' stands for 'specific pathogen-free', not for germ-free husbandry because germ-free animals are in many important ways unnatural.)

In many laboratories the prime qualification for an animal technician was to be proven unfit for any other employment. Advised by our Principal Animal Superintendent, Mr Douglas Short, the MRC saw to it that animal technicians were henceforward trained and properly remunerated and that the highest standards of conventional husbandry were at all times insisted upon. I spent a lot of time preparing a case for submission to the MRC, in the hope that my proposed innovations should be accepted by them as national policy. Although this came about, the fulfilment of these plans was not complete until illness obliged me to give up the Directorship.

Any sufferer from hypomanic busy-ness tends to create the very pressures from which he or she struggles to be free. The condition is self-exacerbating because one tends to be blown up with the feeling of being equal to any demand through having become expert in the allocation and fruitful use of time. It was in this hubristic spirit that I agreed to become the President of the British Association for the Advancement of Science in the year 1969. This entailed a week in the City of Exeter, during the course of which I should be obliged to make twenty-two speeches, presentations, or orations which included the Presidential Address and reading the Lesson at the Association's annual religious service. This last was my undoing, as I shall explain.

Preparing the Presidential Address was rather fun. I decided upon a Baconian title, 'On The Effecting of All Things Possible', my thesis being that science was busily engaged in devising remedies for the many malefactions for which it was alleged to be responsible. In the main this is still a valid thesis, especially if one bears it in mind that many of the malefactions for which science and science-based industry are held responsible, such as the blasting of the countryside in the Black Country in England and around Newark in New Jersey, are in reality the work of nineteenth-century *laissez-faire* capitalism. There is a limit though to what science can do. I have been convinced by the arguments of Amory and Hunter Lovins* that the Western world's energy debauch and use of nuclear energy is building up an inheritance of environmental wrongdoing that science can neither remedy nor expiate.

I enjoyed preparing this lecture and reading the literature bearing upon it, especially Louis Le Roy's *De la Vicissitude ou variété des choses en l'univers*, Condorcet's *Esquisse d'un tableau historique des progrès de l'esprit humain* and other literature relevant to the philosophy of the Enlightenment.† Another good thing the Presidential Address did was to cause me to read much more deeply in the writing of Thomas Hobbes than I had done before. I was greatly helped in this work by the Institute's beautiful library, staffed by people who, unlike many librarians, *wanted* books to be read and never looked as if they were thinking 'Ah, every time one reads a book it does a quantum of damage to the binding.'

Whereas the preparing and delivering of the Presidential Address were very much in my ordinary line of business which caused me no undue stress, reading the Lesson at the annual service in Exeter Cathedral was an unfamiliar activity‡ which apart from all else made me vulnerable to the divine retribution that the punishment theory of illness seems to promise. The Dean of Exeter Cathedral wrote to tell me the biblical passage that was the Lesson for the day. I have only a faint recollection of what this was—something about how the Lord of Hosts would strew over Mount Sinai the bowels of any tribe that opposed the passage of the Israelites into the Holy Land. I was so deeply unedified that I wrote to the Dean and asked what 'lesson' I expected my scientific colleagues to learn from my reading of it? The Dean replied that it would take too long to explain the spiritual meaning of the passage I complained of; if I did not like it he would suggest another passage. This alternative was from the

---

* *Energy/War: Breaking the Nuclear Link* (New York, 1981).

† This lecture may be found in *Pluto's Republic* (Oxford, 1982), 324–39.

‡ Karl Popper teased me about this, saying 'I understand that when your illness struck you, Peter, you were engaged in some religious ceremony.'

Wisdom of Solomon, and I thought it much more suitable for the British Association.

I gave my Presidential Address on Saturday and followed it by standing in for a colleague who failed to arrive to give his lecture. We then went for a scramble on Dartmoor, followed by an extremely cold swim in the river Dart, which I found refreshing—probably because it reduced my blood pressure. But on Sunday morning I felt rather subdued and ill at ease, and when Jean teased me about it I said, 'I am in no mood for raillery or indeed for divine service.'

Illness

While I read the Lesson I became aware that something was going wrong: my speech became slow and rather slurred and I felt as if I was somehow being dragged down on my left side. I completed the Lesson, however, and was supported by a verger back to my place, hoping to look as if nothing was happening. Jean realized that I was having a stroke. She said to the Cathedral dignitary sitting next to her, 'My husband is having a stroke. I must go to him.' He tried to reassure her, 'Don't be concerned, dear lady, it's probably the acoustics.' She boldly came to my seat and I was helped down the aisle and transported as quickly as possible to the Royal Infirmary, where I came under the care of Mr John Simpson FRCS. It was all monstrous bad luck, because at this time Dr Jim Whyte Black had not yet devised beta blockers, which slow the heart-beat and could have preserved my health and my career. As it was, it soon became clear that I had had a massive bleed in my right cerebral hemisphere. As soon as he heard of this disaster, the Professor of Medicine in University College London, Sir Max Rosenheim, who had been advising me, came straight to Exeter. A doctor, Jean, and a nurse took me up to London by train and in accordance with Max Rosenheim's instructions I was transported directly to McAlpine Ward in the Middlesex Hospital, in order to come under the care of Michael Kremer, whom Max rated the foremost neurologist in England. McAlpine was an eight-bedded ward in the charge of Shirley Kean, known through-out the hospital for her expertise as a nurse and, I may add from my own knowledge, her psychological insight and her belief in the efficacy of the form of therapy known as TLC (tender loving care).

A right-sided cerebral haemorrhage impairs the use of the left arm and the left leg, and the left half of each eye. There was also some anxiety about the possibility of mental impairment. Two circumstances put Jean's and my physicians' minds at rest on the subject of my higher faculties. The first was that I had said shortly after my stroke, with reference to my having read the lesson, 'Human beings simply don't realize the risks they run when they meddle in the supernatural.' I learned later that this remark had come to the ears of the Bishop, Dr Mortimer, who was said to have thought it—as I did myself—rather funny. The second piece of evidence was proffered my first night in the Middlesex Hospital after the operation to remove the blood clot from my brain. Jean stayed with me all night because my fate was uncertain. I myself, habitually sanguine, had considered and dismissed the possibility of dying. I was so deeply unconscious after the operation for the removal of the clot that Dr Kremer encouraged Jean to get me to wake up and take notice. She accordingly leaned over, bringing her pretty face close to mine and whispering words to bring me to my senses and say something to her. My first words were 'Entire visual field is agreeably occupied.' I thought this remark apposite and well turned and it repudiated the case that my mind had deteriorated beyond hope of recovery.

Getting better after a stroke is a weary and lengthy business. It is a matter of time more than anything else and of course of the skill of the physiotherapists. In this latter respect I was very well served and marvelled at their patience and willingness to crawl on the floor to pull my left leg for me in my first lessons in walking. I had one frightening setback, though—more than two months after my original operation I developed a violent headache that was judged to be due to a substantial brain abscess caused, it turned out, by bacteria which presumably entered the original wound through the drainage tube necessarily inserted into it. This called for another, very urgent operation, which, not unexpectedly, caused further scarring and neurological damage. My mind wandered a bit after this second operation and I can remember some confused and unreasonable thoughts: I complained urgently to Jean that lying under my bed was an enormous radioactive skate which could not but be a danger to other patients. It was also discovered that I had lost the left half of my field of vision in both eyes. Even this disability made its contribution to the human comedy by making it possible for the more audacious nurses to creep up on the left-hand side of my bed, reach over, and help themselves to chocolate truffles or any of the other delicacies my friends had brought me. My visual defect, incidentally, was identified using the simplest possible apparatus—passing a bunch of jingling keys past my visual field from left to right while I looked straight ahead. My condition was discerned by Dr Graham Bull, a very intelligent and accomplished physician who later became Head of the MRC's Clinical Research Centre and thus in a year or two my boss.

Life in the ward during convalescence was not without its distractions. Jean came for about half of every day, in spite of being preoccupied and harassed by administrative problems in the Family Planning Association of which she was the chairman, bringing nourishing home-made soup ('nerve soup', I called it) and news of the outside world. With Sister Kean's connivance we also kept at bay a number of people who, though I had no wish to see them, wanted to see me, more out of curiosity than compassion. But my true friends and my children—and sometimes theirs—were a joy and they also gave much pleasure to the nurses and other inmates of the ward. With characteristic wisdom Dr Kremer allowed me a modest ration of B and B (Benedictine and Brandy) to recruit my spirits from time to time, and I, having been educated at an English public school, thought hospital food tasty and agreeable and always looked forward to my 'wittles'. Physiotherapy proceeded daily and I enjoyed it when not hopelessly slugged by the injudicious practice of administering sleeping tablets at night.

After four or five months I was judged fit enough to go to a rehabilitation centre that turned out to be the worst medical institution of any kind I have ever known—a tragic example of how what might otherwise have been a good place was morally undermined by a self-important and in my opinion incompetent director. I was taken to this little man for a first appraisal by Jean and a close friend, Dr David Pyke, who was also Registrar of the Royal College of Physicians. I did not look for or expect anything but civility and a sound medical judgement, but this was not to be my lot. The director was evidently much put out by my being a Knight and a Nobel-Prize winner. He'd show me, he must have thought, when he bustled into his office past the three of us, waiting at the appointed time. Instead of saying, as a normal human being would, 'I'll be with you in just a second', he disregarded us completely and stalked into his office. When I entered, the clinical appraisal began. Of my left arm, after a perfunctory examination he said, 'Your arm will never get better: it's not worth my while to prescribe any treatment for it.' The treatment he did prescribe was not, as I had hoped, that I should be given lessons in walking, but that I should have lessons in how to propel a wheelchair using only one arm and one leg. He also arranged for me a psychological appraisal, the design of which was so disgracefully bad it deserves to be recounted in detail. I was sat before an apparatus rather like a typewriter with one row of perhaps fifteen numbered keys alternating in colour. The depression of one of these keys either lit up a cheerful little light-bulb or made the electronic equivalent of a refined fart. The exercise was to traverse the keyboard from left to right depressing as I went along only those keys that would cause the light to come on, eschewing farts. 'Take your time', said the psychologists, 'and have as many goes as you like.' I tried again and again, starting off all right by recognizing a pattern in the colours of the keys but always ending with farts. I became increasingly exasperated and eventually—for this is one of the most disagreeable sequelae of a stroke—rather tearful. The psychologists decided I was mentally impaired and told Jean so—a judgement with which she did not agree, though she might easily have been upset. The truth is that these psychologists did not suspect or look for evidence of the eye defect which should have been as obvious to them as it had been to Graham Bull when he had asked me to draw a man for him—in a matchstick form, if I couldn't do better. I had drawn a matchstick man, gave him a fine head of hair but no right arm or right leg, these being outside my field of vision. Although he had a much better clue than Graham Bull had, the director was not attentive enough to discern that anything was amiss.

The exercises at working a wheelchair with one arm and one leg were in full swing when I had a surprise visit one afternoon from Sister Kean and the head of the Physiotherapy Department at the Middlesex Hospital—a friendly call to see how I was getting on. They were scandalized that I was not walking and that no attempt had been made to teach me to do so. I had indeed deteriorated seriously, having received no treatment whatsoever, though my room-mate—a doctor of science—had been gravely instructed by the occupational therapists in how to toast bread by holding a pre-cut bread slice between forefinger and thumb, dropping it into an electric toaster, and switching on the electric current. It was the kind of toaster, I suspect, that would announce the completion of the operation by playing the 'Star-Spangled Banner' as the toast leapt out of the instrument on to one's plate. The occupational therapists tried to teach me to tie a shoe-lace with one hand but, whether through my stupidity or their inability to teach, it was a knack I never mastered. Living in this remedial centre was a real pain. The male nurses I came across were homosexual to the extent that I dreaded being bathed or conducted to the lavatory by them; I was also dismayed to find when I returned from a weekend at home that the attractive picture of Jean I kept in my bedside drawer to spirit me up from time to time had been neatly torn across, leaving a pile of fragments that could not be reassembled.

Another of the trials of the stroke or MS victim is to hear the views of amateur theologians who see misfortune as a manifestation of divine benevolence. Thus a speaker on BBC Radio 4's popular morning 'God-spot' said that one of the lesser benefactions of a disabling illness was the opportunity it created for others to display magnanimity and helpfulness that would make them feel good. I was not impressed by this argument.

Another indignity I had to submit to was a drawing class where I was required to execute a still life consisting of a bottle of gin (empty) and a glass (the art teacher told Jean 'I always think it does "them" good to do something different'). It didn't do me a bit of good because of my loss of vision and because I am in any case a wholly verbal type with not much visual sense. This episode resolved me to quit the premises, beginning with long weekends at home. My action was strongly opposed by one or two of the psychiatrists with their overall pockets full of anti-depressants. They warned Jean that if I went home even for a weekend I would probably refuse to come back at all. All this determined us to cut short the proposed stay of several months. When Jean informed the director of this, he said grimly, 'On your own head be it.'

My stay at this supposedly remedial centre had been a complete waste of time. The lack of treatment had made me worse and pop music, piped from morning till night, had left me no peace or opportunity for real rest. I was very low indeed after my stay in this ghastly place, having lost my habitual *joie de vivre* and also to a large extent quickness of mind and verbal fluency.

The tearfulness I have referred to is the most embarrassing long-term effect of the stroke, as many other stroke victims have observed. This readiness to dissolve into sobbing is *not* a sign of misery or depression, though goodness knows there is reason enough for it to be so: it is physiological in origin and is not uncommon after extensive injuries to the brain. It is true that sad situations in plays or, characteristically, at the end of operas would provoke weeping—but then, happy endings did also. A moment of glory is a more dangerous trigger than the denouement of a tragedy such as the ending of *Othello*, whether opera or play. As everyone knows, it is an invariable characteristic of tragedy that one feels that all the mischiefs and misunderstandings could be circumvented if only one could join the cast and say a few reassuring words to the principal characters—'Watch out for that Iago,' you whisper urgently, 'he's up to mischief; and by the way don't read any significance into that handkerchief.'

Tragedy is bad enough, God knows, but moments of glory are even worse: in Beethoven's *Fidelio* my undoing is not the miserable plight of the unjustly imprisoned Florestan, but the moment when his faithful wife (alias Fidelio) draws a pistol on the wicked prison governor and distant trumpets from the prison tower announce the arrival of the sheriff's posse—of justice, therefore, and freedom. Fidelio usually gets an ovation at the end of the opera, but my tribute is more often tears—especially if Fidelio is Gwyneth Jones. All this is much more moving then an ostensibly more tragic situation, such as the end of *La Bohème*. The heroine Mimì, surrounded by loving friends, sinks into the last minutes of her life. The extremities are cold, the pulse barely perceptible, and the breathing very light and shallow. Her friends pool and sell their trinkets—one, his overcoat—and propose the preposterous remedy: 'send for some medicine!' This ludicrous suggestion provokes, for a medical scientist, laughter rather than tears. I am pretty sure that Sir William Osler must have heard this Edwardian favourite and I wonder if it gave him cause to question the wisdom of his famous teaching that medicine in his time was totally inefficacious. A cognate situation, as I told the Royal College of Physicians in a brief address on disability, occurs in *La Traviata*, in which the proposed remedy is even more absurd: 'send for a doctor, send for a doctor!' The College seemed to share my delighted amusement and its President proposed a light dose of Mozart.

I went back to full-time work as soon as I reasonably could, and with the support of my staff I went through the motions of being Director. But I felt as if my life had been transposed to a lower key, especially as the loss of the use of my left hand denied me what had until then been the deep pleasure and intellectual stimulus of working at the bench. The great enemy of which I became acutely aware was *tiredness*, and I spent the working day longing for the evening to come and the working week longing for the weekend—this in spite of having lunch in my room and an after-lunch rest, all arranged for me by my secretary Pauline Townend, whose attentiveness and considerateness helped to keep me afloat at this difficult time. Because we were embarking upon a new project in which I specially wanted to play a practical part, I did begin by sitting beside Mrs Ruth Hunt, using my right hand for various delicate technical procedures while she supplied the office of the left hand. This procedure continued, until with great tact and very good sense Ruth delicately intimated to me that we should get on much better and more quickly if she were to do the whole job herself. I gladly accepted her advice and henceforward she became my right hand as well as my left, with the advantages she had foreseen. Although Ruth was classified as a technician in terms of administrative nomenclature, her skill and intelligence had for some time past effectively made her my research assistant. We collaborated well and in 1985 she also qualified for an M.Sc. degree.

Just now the MRC was going through a difficult period. Thanks mainly to the—in my opinion—injudicious advocacy of Lord Rothschild, the government was engaged in reorganizing the funding of the Research Councils on the basis of the retail trade: customer–contractor was to be the principle, in which the scientist was to put up a research proposal to the government and if the government approved, the scientist would be given a contract to undertake it and bring about the desired result. This was a very bold innovation and had not been the basis on which research had hitherto been conducted. Nor was it the proceeding that had given us penicillin, insulin, the discovery of the blood groups, the elucidation of the causes of myasthenia gravis, the transplantation of tissues, or the discovery of the genetic code. Scientific discovery cannot be premeditated.*

With these difficulties impending, the Council not unnaturally thought it would be well for all parties if their oldest and largest research unit were henceforward to be administered by a younger man, physically fit. When I had been recruiting staff in the past, I always made the point of telling them that the Council was a good employer and that if they did well they would be properly looked after. In my case the Council now had a chance to earn the opinion I had formed of them and they rose to the occasion: it was decided to transplant me and those of my immediate colleagues who would accompany me to the Clinical Research Centre, newly built on the site that also housed the big and very well-equipped regional hospital—Northwick Park Hospital, a mile or so from Harrow-on-the-Hill.

This judgement was of course a blow to me but I could see there was a lot of sense in it. I am essentially a managing-director type and newly appointed managing directors usually do any good they are going to do within five years of their appointment, though the fulfilment of their plans is likely to take somewhat longer than that. I had been Director of the National Institute for nine years, during which the talents of its scientific staff had included immunologists of international reputation such as John Humphrey, Ite Askonas, Leslie Brent, Avrion Mitchison, Martin Raff, Elizabeth Simpson, and David Dresser; not to mention a number of scientific guests including Sol Berson, co-discoverer of immuno-electrophoresis, who set us an awe-inspiring example of total commitment to scientific research; Eugene Lance, the orthopaedic surgeon, and my old friend H. Sherwood (Jerry) Lawrence whose endeavour to demonstrate that a cell-free extract might be a vector of cell-mediated immunity I had followed through all its excitements and setbacks for some twenty years, since we had worked together in University

* See my book *The Limits of Science* (New York, 1984; Oxford, 1985).

College. With this galaxy of talent it is not surprising that the NIMR came to rank as the principal centre of immunological research in the world. I had done what I could, therefore, and was in a mood to start on a new life in which, being now relieved of administrative chores which I admit I had found increasingly tiresome, I would be able to devote myself uninterruptedly to research and writing.

Starting Again

The Clinical Research Centre in which the Council had arranged I should henceforward work was another big agency of the Medical Research Council. The CRC was very largely the conception of Sir Harold Himsworth, the Head of the MRC, in close collaboration with Professor John Squire of Birmingham University, the Institute's Director-designate. The conception underlying it was the creation of an environment in which clinically orientated research might be prosecuted with the added advantage of having patients in the immediate neighbourhood. The CRC was thus to be a new and improved embodiment of a notion that had already been expressed on a smaller scale in some of the great teaching hospitals and in one of the country's major centres of excellence for medical research—the Royal Postgraduate Medical School in Hammersmith. The entire enterprise received a sickening blow at the outset with the death of John Squire, whose brilliance as a scientifically minded clinician was acknowledged by all. A man who was also an embodiment of the 'Type A' of Friedman and Rosenman's classification,* Squire was a dynamo of energy and an inveterate smoker, the kind of man of whom laymen tend to say that 'he lives on his nerves'—and on one awful day he died of the coronary attack to which Friedman and Rosenman would have said he was behaviourally predisposed. He was succeeded in the Directorship by Dr Graham Bull, to whom I have already referred in describing my sojourn in the Middlesex Hospital. When Graham Bull retired he was succeeded by Christopher Booth,

* Meyer Friedman and Ray H. Rosenman, *Type A Behavior and your Heart* (New York, 1974). See also my *Pluto's Republic* (Oxford, 1982), 148–53.

the then Professor of Medicine in the Royal Postgraduate Medical School. Dr Booth's dedication to the research idea was not merely notional, for he had made very important contributions to our understanding of malfunctions of the digestive tract. I was treated with the greatest kindness and understanding by both Directors.

My close colleague and friend Eugene Lance had come to us with a high reputation as a surgeon, to which he now added strong evidence of his prowess as a scientist. It was a wise move, then, that he should have been designated head of the Division of Surgical Sciences at the CRC, where he would practise orthopaedic surgery and prosecute medical research— and at the same time keep an eye on me, doing whatever was necessary to keep my head above water if I found life difficult to cope with.

Gene Lance stayed with me until I was once again scientifically viable and self-propelled, and he did this at considerable cost to himself, for his salary was only a fraction of that which he could command in the United States—and it was not sufficient for him to run a household and educate four children.

It was a source of particular pleasure to me that Dr Elizabeth Simpson, whom I have already described as one of the foremost immunologists in England, opted to join me. This was a special pleasure because I had recruited her some years before to the staff of the NIMR and she was a scientist of great ability already well known for her research on the white blood corpuscles known as lymphocytes. She added greatly to the scientific strength and what I called the mateyness of the little group of workers that now set up house in the CRC. Fortunately Mrs Joy Heys, who had been my second secretary at the NIMR, also chose to join and help to organize us, in spite of having to make a very inconvenient journey to do so.

After I got my breath back, I wrote a series of aphorisms on life in hospital, inspired by Katharine Whitehorn's *How to Survive in Hospital* (London, 1972), one of a series of manuals on how to survive in a variety of life-threatening situations.

My aphorisms gave me an opportunity to say something nice in public about the nursing staff at the Middlesex Hospital. American readers will soon see that it was a British National Health Service hospital I had in mind, though I know that much of what I say applies also to private hospitals in America. I append the aphorisms now just as they appeared in the London *Sunday Times*.

Where to be ill. Large teaching hospitals are recommended. Unless privacy is of overriding importance or you really dislike your fellow-men don't go into a private ward. The nursing won't be better than in a public ward, and may easily be much worse. Besides, in a public ward you will be entertained all day by the unfolding of the human comedy and by contemplating what literary people call the Rich Tapestry of Life.

Long stays in hospital. Lying in bed for any length of time is itself a weakening process, as you will soon find when you try to get up. In adequately staffed hospitals, however, physiotherapists will keep your muscles and joints in working order.

An analogous treatment is necessary for the mind. It is a natural tendency of the mind to come to and remain at a complete standstill. This is a principle of Newtonian stature. Prolonged disuse of the brain is also bad for you. Try therefore to think or converse about something other than the exigencies of hospital life and your own piteous plight. Guests come in useful here (see below: *Visitors*) and so do books.

Books. If you are well enough to read books, they are crucially important for entertainment and keeping the mind in working order. Some serious works should therefore be among them. Remember, however, that if you didn't quite follow Chomsky when you were well, there is nothing about illness that can give you an insight into the working of his mind. Do not read a genuinely funny book within a week of having had an abdominal operation. So far from giving you stitches, it will probably deprive you of them. Books should never be so heavy as to impede the ebb and flow of the blood. A slender anthology of selected English aphorisms is strongly recommended. Ten aphorisms are normally reckoned to be equivalent to a quarter of a grain of phenobarbitone, so never take more than twenty aphorisms except under medical supervision.

Sleep. If you sleep all day you must not be aggrieved if you don't sleep all night. If wakeful, don't clamour for sleeping draughts, but take ten selected English aphorisms with a cup of warm milk (see above: *Books*).

Food. The food in hospitals is surprisingly good, but was not intended for people with dainty or fastidious appetites. Be warned that if you eat all day you will become disgustingly obese and thus very properly an object of derision to your friends. Desist, therefore, and give those chocolates to the nurses.

Radio. It is traditional for hospital beds to be equipped with radio outlets that don't work. Test the radio at the earliest opportunity, complain as soon as possible, and go on complaining until somebody does something about it. When the radio works see that kind friends bring in the *Radio Times*. Then you won't have to reproach yourself for missing that talk on the vegetation of Boolooland. Small transistor radios are fine, provided they have an ear monophone attachment.

Sister. Your ward sister—the head nurse of your ward—is well worth knowing and trying to make friends with, because she is an unusually capable and intelligent woman, which is just as well because she is nurse, teacher, administrator, psychotherapist, and everybody's confidante. You are doing well if you manage to make friends with her.

Nurses. The qualities of character that induce young ladies to enter this overworked and underpaid profession are such as to make them specially likeable people. You will almost certainly want to do something to show your appreciation of them. Flowers and profuse gratitude are not very imaginative. It is a fact, however, that nurses are often ravenously hungry after a long day's duty on the wards or soon after coming on duty after a characteristically inadequate breakfast. A supply of biscuits and cheese may be more acceptable and will certainly be more digestible than a pot of hothouse blooms. Another trait which nurses find agreeable is to be visited by a stream of handsome and preferably unmarried sons, cousins, or brothers.

Visitors. Some visitors come because they love you or are genuinely concerned for you, and these you will generally welcome. Others come because they feel they ought to or to indulge their *Schadenfreude*. The latter should be got rid of as quickly as possible. This can be done only by prior arrangement with Sister, who is adept at making unwanted visitors feel, as well as merely being, unwelcome.

The bodily motions. In some wards the nursing staff give the impression of regarding it as a personal affront if the entire great bowel is not evacuated daily. They attach considerably more importance to this than you need (see 'Ritual Purgation', by Professor L. J. Witts in *The Lancet*, 20 February, 1937).

It is a rightly humiliating thought that, in spite of man's ability to reach the moon, no-one has yet designed a bedpan which is not physiologically inept, uncomfortable, and somewhat obscene. The main factor in making physiotherapy supportable is the feeling that ultimately it will equip you to get out of bed yourself and look after your own needs.

Hospitality to guests: drinking. It has been said that the Middlesex Hospital will do anything for you except allow you to park in the forecourt,* and in general the great teaching hospitals were erected at least half a mile from anywhere it is possible to park a car. This means that your visitors when they arrive will be harassed and exhausted and must be offered the drink which (if they have any sense) they will have brought with them. They will probably offer you a drink at the same time, but as the words 'Thanks, I don't mind if I do' rise to your lips, remember the medical staff may easily mind quite a lot. They certainly will if you are suffering from a serious liver disorder. If your complaints are merely orthopaedic they are not likely to object at all. But here again consult with the ward sister. Tell her, if need be, that you get a funny sort of dizzy swimming feeling in the head if you don't have a drink at six o'clock.

---

* Blessed with the gift of tongues, my beloved Jean was able so skilfully to simulate an Irish lilt that she was authorized to park in the forecourt by the Irish attendant who rebutted all others.

Serious illness: the will to live. A well-known public figure who has taken it upon himself to become the Conscience of the World has objected to organ transplantation as an unnatural and somewhat unwholesome method of prolonging life. But before they insist too vehemently upon the Right to Die, such people should remember that a very decided preference for remaining alive has been a major motive force with human, as with all animal evolution. The firm determination to remain alive has a mysterious therapeutic effect which helps to promote that very ambition.

The National Health Service. Don't run down the National Health Service which, in spite of faults which are inevitable in any man-made scheme, represents the most enlightened piece of social legislation of the past 150 years. If you think you can do better ás a private patient attending private clinics, then good luck to you. You may need it.

I had plenty of time, of course, to think about future research topics. I decided against further research on the scientific basis of organ transplantation because transplantation was not in progress at Northwick Park Hospital and a later proposal that it should be so was turned down on reasonable grounds. Also, I felt I had already made my contribution to the theory of the subject and wanted to turn my thoughts to other things. Because I was aware of some unfinished business in the area of transplantation research I made my decision to abandon it with some reluctance. My discovery of immunological tolerance had, as I have said, a dramatic moral effect on the fraternity of scientists and surgeons who so much wished transplantation therapy to succeed. But the widespread and rather simplistic illusion that my colleagues' and my research on transplantation laid the foundations for organ transplantation as it has been practised for the last ten or twenty years is a mistaken attribution: transplantation of kidneys and subsequently of other organs was introduced by a number of sanguine, adventurous, and skilful surgeons in France, America, and Great Britain by making use of drugs that diminished the immunity that is responsible for graft rejection, without reducing it to a level that might dangerously impair protective immunity against micro-organisms.

I would have liked to investigate the origin of the layer of tissue—the vascular endothelium—that forms the internal lining of the arteries, veins, and lymphatics in successful and long-lived transplants. The conventional belief is that this tissue renews itself when necessary by cell division, as it does in the lining of the gut. I had a hunch that the vascular endothelium was not formed in this way, but originated from elements circulating in the bloodstream and deposited from it. How else can we account for the fact that even inert (that is, orlon or other plastic) tubes used to repair blood vessels are found soon to be lined internally by a vascular endothelium, often from the middle outwards—and not, as conventional theory would lead one to expect, by the ingrowth of endothelium from one end or the other? I propounded my hypothesis before a gathering of vascular surgeons at Wayne State University Medical School in 1984 and was pleased to learn that some members of my audience had been thinking on very much the same lines. Both parties were pleased to learn this, because the camaraderie of science welcomes support for the riskier hypotheses—and on these occasions considerations of priority thought to prey on scientists' minds take an altogether second place. However, I gave up the thought of going deeply into this problem because I could not have the fun of participating myself and it lay too far to one side of the interests of my co-workers.

The two topics upon which I did decide to work both came under the general heading of experimental cancer research. The first was the idea of *immunopotentiation*, that is to say, of strengthening that arm of immunological response which is widely believed to provide a natural defence against the inception and progress of malignant growths. Besides Eugene Lance, there were two young surgeons among my little team at the CRC, John Castro, a urologist, and David Hamilton, a transplant surgeon, and we quite soon made interesting observations on the boosting of the immune response: Castro found that the castration of male mice at puberty—which deprives them of the male hormone—led to hypertrophy of the thymus and lymph nodes and significantly heightened resistance against chemically induced tumours; the effect was counteracted by the administration of testosterone and of antithymocyte serum, the drug upon which Eugene Lance and I had already been working for the preceding three or four years. This reminds me to add that I joined in with and did whatever I could to promote Eugene Lance's research on the use of immunosuppressive agents, particularly anti-thymocyte serum, for the treatment of multiple sclerosis. I had learned enough about its effects to make me feel I would rather be associated with its cure or amelioration than with any other advance in medicine or surgery. This antithymocytic treatment was based on our belief that MS is an autoimmune disease, that is, a disease in which the body reacts immunologically to one of its own constituents as if it were foreign. Multiple sclerosis is a self-exacerbating disease, because no matter how it is triggered the immune response in MS is directed against the myelin sheath of nerves. This causes more damage which further reinforces the immun-ological response.

The trials were followed with great interest and we were helped particularly by the Director of the CRC and by the doyen of British neurologists, Dr Michael Kremer. The results of Eugene Lance's trial, and its continuation by Dr Jürgen Mertin after Lance left, were not conclusive, but were encouraging enough to make us think it should be repeated, perhaps with new and more effective immunosuppressive agents, either of the conventional kind or in the form of monoclonal antibodies directed against one or other of the hormones that activate lymphocytes.

People who adopt a nihilistic attitude towards such attempted remedies—'It's sure not to work'—illustrate just that kind of despondency that Francis Bacon once eloquently denounced as one of the principal impediments to the advancement of learning in his day. In the Preface to his *Great Instauration* Bacon described them as 'men not excited either out of desire or hope to penetrate further'. A despondent spirit is certainly a brake upon the advancement of learning whether by one's self or one's colleagues—for despondency in a laboratory is infectious, while a sanguine temper and a habit of hopeful expectation are among the marks of a successful scientist.

It was an important moment in the administrative history of the MRC when Dr James Gowans FRS, head of one of the Council's smaller units, in Oxford, succeeded Sir John Gray as its head. The moral effect of this appointment was felt throughout the Council's scientific service: now for the first time the big chief was a scientist of world rank—a man who had been nominated for the award of the Nobel Prize by Howard Florey and myself for the discovery of the circulation of lymphocytes. Before Jim Gowans took office, I told him how delighted we all were at his giving up a cushy job as a gentleman–scientist in Oxford to do a real job of work. I went on to discourse eloquently on my plans for research in the areas of immunopotentiation and on the relation between the immunity-provoking substances found in embryos and in malignant cells. Jim Gowans listened patiently for several minutes, smiled and, inspired by an edict of the current Minister of Health, said 'Of course, Peter, you don't realize that you people are all going to be retrained to study lower back pain and nocturnal enuresis.'

The research that I now began followed up a chance discovery Ruth Hunt and I had made while we were still working at the NIMR. If mice were fed for a week or two upon a diet of commercial 'mouse cake' heated to about 120 °C by steam under pressure, they became highly reactive immunologically and threw off skin grafts transplanted from mice of different strains much more vigorously than mice reared upon the conventional diet. Moreover they were much more resistant to the inception of tumours by the potent cancer-causing chemical 3-methylcholanthrene. From this observation I was led by what I can now clearly see to have been a series of unsound inferences to form the opinion that certain derivatives of vitamin A have the power to boost the immunological response—or, to put it more grandiloquently, to exercise immunopotentiation. A Swiss scientist, Dr W. Bollag, had already shown this property to be possessed by an oxidation product of retinol, namely retinoic acid, and one of the NIMR's most distinguished immunologists, Dr David Dresser, had also shown that vitamin A itself could confer upon substances that would not otherwise possess it the power to arouse immunological reactions. A number of American scientists, notably Dr Michael Sporn and Dr Richard Moon, had already been thinking on the same lines.

The whole area of research looked promising and we decided to follow it up, choosing for special investigation the compound vitamin A acetate, retinyl acetate. Retinyl acetate had the further advantage that a well-known drug company dispensed it in a form especially easy to administer to experimental animals. We had no difficulty in confirming and exemplifying its power to potentiate the kind of immunity that is responsible for the rejection of foreign transplants and also, it is believed, to delay the inception and subsequent progress of virally or chemically induced tumours. We made some encouraging observations to begin with: the administration to mice of vitamin A acetate as a supplement to their ordinary diet enlarged the thymus and lymphoid organs generally. We already knew that lymphoid hypertrophy and the immunopotentiation that went with it was annulled by the administration of an antithymocyte serum, so there could be little doubt the problem we were investigating was immunological in character. We were joined now by a Czechoslovak biologist who had formerly been a colleague of Milan Hašek's. We asked him to study what vitamin A acetate was doing to the lymphoid system; he found that its administration increased disproportionately the number of lymphoid cells that are associated with the manufacture of a lymphocyte-stimulating hormone Interleukin II. Indeed, the direct administration of Interleukin II itself exercised many of the effects that could be produced by adding vitamin A acetate to the diet.

This work was interesting enough scientifically and

promising enough in terms of clinical use to justify Council's support of its being continued, as indeed it is. It may well be asked by many investigators why I chose to work upon vitamin A acetate, the ester, instead of pure vitamin A, the alcohol retinol. One reason is that retinol is a somewhat toxic substance—as everyone knows who makes a habit of feasting intemperately off the livers of polar bears.

It is not the most important research work we are currently engaged upon, but I recount it in some detail because it is so characteristic of the way a research project starts and takes shape. It is also characteristic of the international cross-connections that are quickly built up with fellow-workers all over the place who enter the research field through different portals and proceed with different motives in mind. This collaborative expertise, though sometimes—much less often than is thought—marred by rivalry, is one of the great strengths of science and a principal attraction of scientific life.

Embryos and Cancer

The second of the two projects that have occupied my little research team for the past three or four years concerns the affinity between embryonic cells, or adult cells retaining embryonic characteristics, and the cells of malignant tumours.

The belief that there is such an affinity is an inheritance from the bad old days of the German nature-philosophers—for many of them were convinced of the deep kinship between embryonic cells and tumour cells. Virchow's pupil Julius Cohnheim was the man most closely associated with this conception: he believed that the transformation of a normal to a malignant cell was accompanied by a regression or de-differentiation to the embryonic condition. Or, in Cohnheim's view, tumours might arise from embryonic cells which, having somehow got misplaced or left over in the course of development, had become the seeds of tumours that burgeon in adult life. There was precious little evidence for these views at the time they were propounded. To begin with, dedifferentiation does not normally accompany transformation from normal to malignant cells: thus tumours of the melanocytes, that manufacture the colouring matter of skin, continue to manufacture black pigment; tumours of thyroid cells often continue to produce the characteristic secretion of the thyroid gland; and tumours of cells that would normally have formed blood proteins continue to form them. Embryonic cells, moreover, though they do indeed proliferate rapidly, do not possess the most dangerous characteristic of malignant cells: they are not invasive.

It was nearly a hundred years before Canadian and Russian research workers hit upon evidence that seemed to uphold the nature-philosophers' conception of an affinity between embryonic and malignant cells. It was discovered that tumours arising from cells that form the internal lining of the digestive tract frequently manufacture anew the chemical that is also manufactured in the gut cells of foetuses. This is the famous 'carcino-embryonic antigen', CEA. Likewise G. I. Abelev, Russia's principal cancer-research worker, and Y. S. Tatarinov discovered that liver cancers in mice and human beings were manufactured by alpha feto-protein, a substance characteristic of the body fluids of the embryos of vertebrates.

Very many examples are now known of this phenomenon, in which genes that had been active in embryonic life reawaken in tumour cells; these genes normally programme the manufacture of characteristically embryonic substances and cease to work when they have fulfilled their function. They then take their place in the so-called 'silent genome', that part of the genetic apparatus which no longer has a functional expression. I have proposed that we reserve the word 'anaplasia' for this phenomenon of the reawakening in tumour cells of genes that had worked in embryonic or foetal life; the word formerly referred to the phenomenon of dedifferentiation which can no longer be said to occur.

This is one half of a story which, taken with its other half, can raise the possibility of a new and different strategy of approach to cancer.

This other half is the phenomenon of anti-embryo immunity, but in a form somewhat different from the familiar anti-embryo immunity which arises when the foetus immunizes the mother that bears it, because it possesses alien substances programmed by genes inherited from the father. A typical example is the hemolytic disease of the new-born that sometimes arises in later pregnancies from unions between a Rhesus-positive man and a Rhesus-negative woman; the rhesus antigen being foreign to the mother and therefore capable of provoking an immunological response that reacts upon red blood corpuscles of the infant.

This is *not* the kind of phenomenon I have in mind when I refer to anti-embryo immunity (which often takes a different and more general form). It is more often an immunity directed against embryonic cells *as such*; for foetuses considered as organisms are very different from the adults into which they grow up. Foetuses are organisms adapted to life in a uterine environment and specialized accordingly. I want to stress that embryos are sufficiently unlike the adults into which they develop to be able to arouse in them an immunological reaction, against the embryo *as an embryo* and not against the embryo as an object partially foreign to the mother by reason of the characteristics inherited from its father. We have now to compound two well-authenticated phenomena: 1. *anaplasia*, the reappearance of embryonic substances in tumour cells themselves and 2. *anti-embryo immunity*, the immunological response aroused in mothers by their embryos as a result of their possessing specialized, characteristically embryonic substances that are foreign to the mother.

A crucial inference now follows: if embryos contain these distinctive immunity-provoking substances, antigens, and *if* the phenomenon of anaplasia in the malignant cells extends to the reawakening of genes that programme and specify the manufacture of these immunity-provoking embryonic antigens, then should not tumours also arouse in their subjects an immunity that is essentially an anti-embryo immunity and, conversely, should not a deliberately provoked anti-embryonic immunity confer some resistance to the inception and growth of tumours?

The second question is the more important and the answer is 'Yes, it should do so'—and it does: inoculation of a variety of embryonic cells into mice does to quite a high degree protect them against the inception and growth of tumours aroused by inoculation with cancer-producing chemicals or cancer-causing viruses.

I have outlined a tidy logical argument—but as a rule scientific discoveries do not grow out of tidy logical arguments. These elaborate feats of ratiocination come later, to justify or make sense of something already known to be the case. The fact is that protective action against tumours aroused by inoculations of embryonic cells into adults had already been discovered a good many years ago by experiments that must have had a motivation quite different from that which I have just outlined. I cite a long roll of honour that includes names well known in the field of research on the experimental pathology of tumours, excluding the names of my immediate colleagues: Peter Alexander, Norman Anderson, Richard Baldwin, David Billington, Edward Boyse, Joseph Coggin, George Klein, Hilary Koprowski, Lloyd Old, George Schoene.

My team and I have mainly studied the effect of inoculating rats or mice with embryonic cells to protect them from tumours aroused by cancer-causing chemical compounds; we discovered a good deal about the power of the embryonic cells to protect the mice against tumours aroused by 3-methylcholanthrene and dinitrobenzanthracene. One such discovery is especially relevant to the interpretation (given below) of the epidemiology of breast cancer. This discovery was of the prevalence of the phenomenon of *enhancement*—the promotion or facilitation of tumour growth that occurs under certain special circumstances. Tumour protection by inoculation of embryo cells occurs *only* when the protective inoculum of embryonic cells is administered *before* the inoculation of tumour-causing chemicals. If the order is reversed and the tumour-causing chemical is administered first and the would-be protective inoculum of embryonic cells afterwards, the result is enhancement of tumour growth.

There seems no doubt that the phenomenon of heightened resistance to tumours we have been studying is immunological in character: circulating antibodies are formed and the tumour destruction is accompanied by the local congregation of lymphocytes. Moreover, the reaction aroused by the inoculation of embryonic tissues can be made to perform as a hypersensitivity reaction of the delayed type—a well-known feature of the immunological response. Our most interesting finding so far has been that cells from the testis and thymus can also arouse a protective reaction against tumours.

One of the most agreeable features of this work for me has been the chance to team up again with my old colleague Leslie Brent, now Professor of Immunology in St Mary's Hospital Medical School, London. Brent and his team studied the antibodies aroused by the injection into adult mice of embryonic cells and found that they reacted not only upon embryonic cells themselves but also to a significant degree upon testicular and thymic cells.* This degree of overlap in embryonic, testicular, and thymic tissue made it intelligible that these other tissues should also arouse anti-tumour immunity.

Work on the affinity between immunity-provoking substances—'antigens'—in cancerous and embryonic cells put it into our power to proffer a rational explanation of certain already well-known findings on the relationship between a woman's reproductive history and her risk of contracting breast cancer. It has long been known that there is some connection between a woman's *parity*, that is the number of children she has ·had, and her risk of contracting breast cancer. It was at one time thought the higher a woman's parity the lower her chances would be of getting breast cancer, but Dr Brian MacMahon, the head of the Epidemiology Department in the Harvard School of Public Health, showed that the most important independent variable was not the

---

* L. Brent, R. Hunt, I. V. Hutchinson, P. B. Medawar, L. Palmer, and L. Welsh, 'Host recognition of antigens: do they induce specific antibodies?' in *Fetal antigens and Cancer*, Ciba Foundation Symposium 96 (London 1983); and P.B. Medawar and R. Hunt, 'Can fetal antigens be used for prophylactic immunization?', ibid.

number of pregnancies a woman has had, but the age at birth of the first child (the age of the *mother*, of course). MacMahon's findings showed that the younger the mother on the birth of her first child, the lower would be her risk of subsequently contracting breast cancer. Taking the cancer risk of a childless woman as the base line, a woman who bore her first child as a teenager is about half as likely as she is to contract breast cancer. But a woman whose first child was born when she was thirty or upwards is at decidedly *greater* risk of contracting breast cancer than a childless woman. The truth of MacMahon's findings is not in question but their interpretation is controversial: endocrinologists (the medical scientists who study hormones and the glands that secrete them) are inclined to an endocrinological explanation, whereas immunologists, such as I am, lean equally strongly towards an immunological explanation. Medical students, being young enough to be cynical, laugh rather contemptuously at this tendency of specialists to interpret medical phenomena in terms of their own speciality, and so, in my experience, do those administrators with little experience of scientific research. But there should be nothing funny in the inclination of endocrinologists and immunologists to interpret phenomena in the light of their own specialities. 'Light' is a key word. All experienced scientists know that *one must seek where the light is*. Immunology and endocrinology are brightly lit domains of medical science and it would be the height of folly not to seek first in their own well-lit fields.

Ruth Hunt and I* believed that an early first pregnancy is essentially a vaccination that confers cross-protection against cancer. The strength of this immunological interpretation is its appeal to a phenomenon easy to demonstrate in the laboratory, namely the extra protection conferred upon rats and mice by passage through a pregnancy, something demonstrated in experimental animals by both Dr Richard Moon in the US and my Ugandan Asian colleague Dr Dominic Pinto. Moreover, the immunological interpretation accounts satis-

* P. B. Medawar and R. Hunt, 'Vulnerability of methylcholanthrene-induced tumours to immunity aroused by syngeneic foetal cells', *Nature*, cclxxi (1978), 164.

factorily for the apparent anomaly that older first mothers are more at risk of breast cancer than younger mothers. This, in our estimation, illustrates the working of the ubiquitous phenomenon of enhancement, for example when supposedly protective vaccination is administered *after* the injection of a cancer-causing chemical, and the tumours arise more quickly and grow more rapidly. The immunological interpretation still satisfies me, but it is always possible, of course, that some quite different and so far unsuspected set of factors is at work.

I have outlined the subjects upon which my immediate colleagues and I have been working since 1970 when I returned to the laboratory after my first CVA (cerebral vascular accident), and thanks to the magnanimity of the MRC we are working upon them still. Magnanimity, because in a technical administrative sense I have long since 'retired'. Indeed, I have already had two agreeable farewell parties organized by my friends and colleagues. Neither was intended as or interpreted as a gentle hint that it was time I took my *congé* and left the field to others.

The first party took the form of a symposium of papers delivered by former friends and colleagues on the topics that had interested us all so deeply—a party organized by Professors Jerry Lawrence and Leslie Brent. The meeting was chaired by Sir James Gowans and it was followed by a dinner party honoured by the presence of two of the greatest modern Englishmen—Sir Karl Popper and Sir Ernst Gombrich—close friends and both as it happens born in Vienna of Jewish families who had fled from political tyranny. Karl Popper is in my opinion the world's foremost living philosopher, and Sir Ernst Gombrich is the wisest and most learned man I have ever known.

My second farewell was back at the Clinical Research Centre—a supper party given by my closest colleagues. In the thanks that followed it, thinking of an old hero of mine, Sir D'Arcy Wentworth Thompson, I told the company that it was my ambition to continue working until I too had become a notorious abuse. I hope to continue working, I said, until as

I career down the corridors in my electric wheelchair, new-comers flattening themselves against the wall will say to each other 'That's Medawar, you know: they simply can't get rid of him.' 'We're saying that already, Peter!' amiably called Christopher Booth, from his end of the supper table.

I had foreseen that I should want if possible to continue with research, and on the subject of growing older I had written as follows in my *Advice to a Young Scientist* (1979):

> Like any other human being, a young scientist growing up will probably say to himself at the end of each decade, 'Ah well, that's it, then. It has all been great fun, but nothing now remains except to play out time with dignity and composure and hope that some of my work will last a bit longer than I do.'
>
> Such dark thoughts are wider of the mark with scientists than with most other people. No working scientist ever thinks of himself as old, and so long as health, the rules of retirement, and fortune allow him to continue with research, he enjoys the young scientist's privilege of feeling himself born anew every morning. Their infectious zest was one of the most endearing characteristics of that great generation of American biologists on whose behalf all ordinary laws of mortality and even the physical intimations of it seemed to have been held in abeyance: Peyton Rous (1879–1970), G. H. Parker (1864– 1955), Ross G. Harrison (1870–1959), E. G. Conklin (1863– 1952), and Charles B. Huggins (1901–   ).

It would be an unanswerable argument in favour of retiring if by not doing so I were an obstacle to the advancement of others, but I am not so: my administrative position as a sectional head was taken over by my loyal colleague and friend Dr Elizabeth Simpson. She is no more oppressed by administrative duties than I ever was, because at the CRC administration is conducted by professional administrators who are as good at their jobs as the scientific staff believe themselves to be at theirs.

JEAN

The ultimate sentence of an obituary notice in *The Times* often takes the following form: 'In 1839 he married Emma, youngest daughter of Josiah Wedgwood of Meare Hall, by whom he had ten children.' And that's it: so much for what might have been half a lifetime's companionship, and for the shared joys or sorrows that are the landmarks of married life. If I were a woman and not yet a feminist, this graceless and perfunctory form of words would assuredly have made me so.

Jean Shinglewood Taylor, whom I was to marry, was the daughter of a Cambridge physician and a half-American mother who had been born in St Louis, Missouri. Charles Henry Shinglewood Taylor, Jean's father, although a man of slight build, was an oarsman who had stroked the Cambridge crew to victory over Oxford and upon graduation in medicine made a speciality of looking after the oarsmen. He was a man of gentle and unassertive disposition with very many admiring friends to whom he was affectionately known as 'Joss', after Joshua Taylor, a well-known firm of outfitters in Cambridge. Joss's friends made up between them an impressive cadre of honorary uncles—a mixed blessing, though Jean remained friends with some of them all her life, especially Hamish Hamilton the publisher and Harold Abrahams the athlete. With a degree of judgement remarkable in one so young she decided to study at Oxford—not, as might have seemed natural, at Cambridge. She did well at school and won a scholarship to Somerville College to study zoology; so it was as fellow-students of zoology that we met. Jean Taylor was the most beautiful woman student in Oxford—though hers was a generation of students notable for the quality Americans refer to as 'pulchritood'. I fell in love with her, of course; but I did not meet her much socially because I was a not very well-off student and we tended to move in different circles. It was philosophy that brought us together. Because of my own interest in the subject, Jean one day came to me shyly to ask the meaning of the word 'heuristic'—a word which laymen more often look up and more often forget than any other in the philosophic vocabulary.

I was delighted by this evidence of Jean's awakening interest in philosophic matters. I accordingly offered to give her tutorials on such matters as mechanism, vitalism, and other quasi-philosophic aspects of biology, teaching her on very much the lines that subsequently became our 'philosophic dictionary of biology', *Aristotle to Zoos*. Jean agreed, and we arranged to meet now and again at my lodgings, at that time in the Iffley Road. She did not lead an exuberantly social life and was not a great party-goer. Indeed, if drinks were proffered she more often than not chose milk. She thus had no kind of head for alcoholic refreshments, something I was not aware of. After one tutorial I offered her one—nay, two—glasses of sherry. Although sherry is regarded as a kid's drink by those folk whose habitual tipple is a Martini or Manhattan cocktail, it is in fact quite intoxicating and when the time came to take her home, Jean was so sure that the swimming feeling in her head was betraying itself in her outer behaviour that she turned to me with characteristic sweetness and said 'Shall I make a remark?' 'No, for Jesus' sake, don't', I said: and this was the only time in my life I have ever known her at a disadvantage from alcohol. About twenty years later she and I, with our son Charles, went to Czechoslovakia where I was fulfilling an engagement to lecture at the Institute of the Czechoslovak Academy of Sciences. One evening, Charles, Jean, and I were chatting with our Czech friends after dinner in a hotel in the Tatra mountains and bottle after bottle of wine was brought to our table. We could see that we were to take part in one of the grimmest central European social observances—'Why, we sat up all night talking and drinking.' I was still in a delicate state from an allergic illness brought on by the administration of penicillin, so pleading indisposition I retired to bed. Jean and Charles, however, conscious that the honour of England was now in the balance, opted to stick it out a lot longer and they did not return to our rooms until more than an hour later, both arriving absolutely exhausted. The fact that they did not 'fwow up', as Beatrice Lillie used to say, until they reached the privacy of their rooms, meant that the Union Jack was still fluttering aloft.

One other evening during this visit, Milan Hašek invited us home for an evening meal, for which purpose we all packed into a tiny Simca which Milan intrepidly drove into a deep trench in the road. Jean's face was badly bashed, a canine tooth of Charles's was pushed through his cheek, and I had a jagged cut on the forehead from which blood was streaming out. A little ambulance was summoned into which I was pushed. In the mean time an obviously drunken spectator had come to the scene of the accident to give himself the pleasure of witnessing the drama: he himself then fell into the trench and was also pushed into the ambulance. In hospital the wound on my forehead was stitched up in an inept operation that included some of my long front hairs. No local anaesthetic was administered: such drugs, I was told, were deemed to be injurious to the *organism*, so once again the Union Jack fluttered aloft as I put up uncomplainingly with the maladroit operation of suture without anaesthetic. I had an X-ray, too, just to be sure. What became of the little man who came to see the accident I never heard. We looked a proper fright when we left the hospital and very soon after we decided to drive home. Every time we stopped for a little shopping or a meal everyone averted their gaze and at no time was mention made of the fact that we all looked as if we had been beaten up. Perhaps such a sight was so commonplace as to be thought unworthy of remark. When we reached the frontier we found it heavily fortified and we observed, as many others have done, that the defences, especially massive barbed-wire fencing, were all directed inwards as they would be in a prison, which, in effect, Czechoslovakia was. The current joke was that it would be supererogatory to defend the frontiers as if people wanted to come in—for who would want to enter Czechoslovakia? What people wanted was to get out.

But I am running away with myself and must return now to my rather sordid room in the Iffley Road. I made up my mind to propose to Jean at one of our meetings, but I was completely lacking in social self-assurance and had no reason to expect that I should be accepted. My clothes were bought from the cheapest outfitters in England, 'The Fifty Shilling Tailors', and I wore artificial silk shirts bought at Marks and Spencer's. I had a frightening memory of having once been invited by a schoolfellow to have lunch with him and a rather posh aunt at her elegant flat, an occasion on which I could not muster the social technique to get up and go when it was time to do so. It sounds so easy: one rises to one's feet, thanks one's hostess graciously for her hospitality, says it is high time to leave, and does so. Unfortunately no favourable opportunity presented itself and so through sheer ineptitude I stayed on in agony for at least an hour after I should have left. Incidents such as these had undermined my social confidence and made me more diffident than I need have been in making my proposal, but it soon came to be agreed between us that we were destined for each other and we resolved to get married as soon as we could after Jean had graduated. Our engagement was greeted with consternation by Jean's immediate family and by her honorary uncles, one of whom seized the opportunity to do me a grave disservice—as I shall now recount.

Jean and I went in a jolly party to Oxford's annual St Giles' fair, at which one of the attractions was a slide down a well-polished helical wooden chute. This had been so hastily assembled that a nail was left sticking out near the bottom. This tore my jacket and cut the bursa of my left elbow (the bursa being the bit of loose skin that enfolds the serous sac housing the elbow joint). Next day we went swimming in an indoor pool which I remember today as a dilute solution of sodium hypochloride. From this foolhardy exploit I contracted a severe pyrogenic infection of my elbow—an embarrassment, because I was now to spend a few days at Jean's home in Cambridge and meet her father for the first time. In the outcome I never met him, for he was too ill at the time to receive me, being the victim of bronchitis that was to prove fatal.

In spite of receiving some well-meaning treatment by a local GP, my elbow got worse. Through the good offices of one of Jean's honorary uncles, a Dr Brehmer Heald, it was arranged that I should be taken into the Royal Free Hospital at Gray's Inn Road in London, at which Heald was a consultant in physical medicine. Here he arranged all manner of physical treatments all of which were totally inefficacious, there being no theoretical reason to suppose that they would be otherwise. Among them were 'ionization'—a treatment in which the 'affected part', as physicians say, was treated as the anode of an electrolytic cell in a bath of one per cent sodium chloride, the supposition being that the 'nascent' chlorine formed at the anode had a uniquely potent bactericidal power. Another treatment was to expose my elbow to a tremendous dose of ultraviolet irradiation, a procedure which through no fault of Dr Heald's did me no harm. In addition X-ray photographs were taken of my legs for reasons that will be clear in a moment.

The fact that the infected wound had not responded to his physical–medical treatments, combined with his deep antipathy to the idea of my marrying Jean, caused a new diagnosis of surpassing idiocy to enter his mind—the granulating wound on my elbow, he now opined, was a syphilitic chancre. Poor physician that he was, he fell in love with this idea and was not to be reasoned out of it. How common was it, I asked, for syphilis to be acquired from a heavily chlorinated swimming pool? Not very likely, he conceded; but then might I not perhaps have been 'romping with girls in the Tropics?' I think I was able to satisfy him on this point, but not easily, for Dr Heald, who clearly had the mind of a schoolboy, thought 'the Tropics' connoted some sort of steamy Venusberg full of promiscuous women, all afflicted by tropical and venereal diseases. He added for full measure that the X-rays of my legs had shown a thickening of the tibiae which was not inconsistent with my having been a victim of syphilis. Heald now yielded the centre of the stage to a surgeon who was to excise my infected wound and complete the repair by primary suture of the edges. I remember nothing about the surgeon, Mr Norbury, except that he had only one leg, a feature which cannot, I think, be the reason why, on excising the granuloma, he reinfected the wound created by its excision with, presumably, the same organisms as before. The tissue removed was sent to a pathologist who found that its appearance was consistent with the idea of syphilis. I insisted on seeing him and telling him the whole story of my injury; I asked him what the diagnostic features were of a syphilitic lesion and went on to ask him whether a wound formed in the way mine had been formed might not in some respect simulate a syphilitic lesion. The professor was shaken by my insistent enquiries, which made it clear to both of us how flimsy were the foundations of his beliefs, and he ended up by equivocating to a degree which satisfied me that the idea of syphilis would not have occurred to him in the first place had it not been put to him in the form of a question such as the '?syphilis' which I saw on one of the clinical papers relating to my case. All this amused Jean and me very much, especially Heald's references to 'goings-on in the Tropics'. But one person who was not at all amused was Professor Howard Walter Florey, my then boss to whom with some anxiety I told the whole story. Florey, characteristically, became quite pink with indignation as I told him all and eventually he said he would try to arrange to get a sensible opinion; he began by sending me up to London to the consulting rooms of a distinguished radiologist whom he had briefed. After looking amusedly at the X-rays of my legs, the consultant said 'I expect you play rugby football, don't you?' So that was the last of that silly damn nonsense. But what a disgraceful and discreditable story; and it was alarming to imagine what harm such incompetence might do among patients who were not well able to defend themselves.

Our marriage was resolutely opposed by Jean's family.

'What will you do if you have black babies?' Jean's mother asked her; and the marriage was also opposed by one of her sisters, whose thoughts had been shaped by the novels of Dornford Yates, in which wealthy and debonair characters went purring around in six-cylinder cars from one posh restaurant to another—restaurants patronized by 'exquisitely gowned' women and yuppy young men with gold cigarette cases. Jean told me that this sister's principal objection to her marrying me was that I would not be able to go into such a restaurant and order a meal as she imagined Dornford Yates's characters would. Jean's American aunt also opposed the match. She had a loud voice and was an irremediable snob. She had insisted that the children address her as *tanta*, instead of aunt, but childish lips rebelled at this absurdity and she accordingly came to be called Tatan. Our proposed marriage was a great disappointment to her—I had no background, no money, she said. She threatened to cut Jean off without a penny and did so.

We were married anyway in February of 1937. One of our closest friends throughout this time was a young German refugee Louis 'Budi' Hagen, an attractive and brave young man who later enlisted in the Pioneer Corps, becoming eventually a glider pilot. In this capacity he received a field award of the Military Medal for conspicuous bravery at the battle of Arnhem, about which he wrote a marvellous little book (*Arnhem Lift*) soon rated a minor classic of war literature. Budi was very keen that we should spend our honeymoon at his father's splendid lakeside home in Potsdam, the headquarters of his private bank, one of the largest in Germany.

The Hagens had extensive literary and theatrical connections and they gave a big party for us, attended by two of Germany's most famous actors, Gustav Gründgens and Werner Krauss. I did not cut a very impressive figure at this party, not so much because I do not speak German as because I do not understand it. Jean more than made up for my shortcomings; because as I moved from one room to another I came upon one in which she was clearly holding court, surrounded by an absolutely delighted group of smiling spectators to whom she was recounting a dialect joke in German ('God, what a nerve!' I thought to myself). Jean told me afterwards that one of the reasons why the audience was so amused was because she told her story in the rather prim manner she had picked up from the Freiburg landladies with whom she had learnt her German some years beforehand when she had spent two months in Germany listening to the lectures of the great embryologist Professor Hans Spemann. After our German honeymoon Jean and I returned to an Oxford darkened by the understanding that the outbreak of a Second World War was waiting only upon Hitler's convenience, a disagreeable environment in which to raise a family, as we hoped to do. I remember most vividly one aspect of our preparations for war: almost weekly articles in the *New Statesman and Nation* were written to illustrate our defencelessness against the bomber. The coast of England, the *New Statesman* reasoned, was such and such a distance from the coast of Holland. Modern bombers, moreover, travelled at so many miles an hour, and a simple division sum would accordingly make it clear that the bombers must be upon us before our plucky fighter planes could take to the air, and so on. The author seemed quite unable to conceive that these simple syllogisms might also have entered the minds of men of science or men of war. This was of course the danger that begat radar—a subject about which I, a biologist, knew nothing; my attempts to find out something about the mysterious coastal stations springing up round the coast of England were rebuffed skilfully and politely by Henry Tizard and Dr James Griffiths of Magdalen, both of whom knew all about them. At the beginning of the war Jean and I, Howard Florey and his wife, and other Oxford families, attended a grim meeting in Rhodes House to decide whether or not we wished to send our wives and/or children to the generous American families who had offered to take them in. Howard Florey sent his children to John and Lucia Fulton in New Haven, but we decided that if we were going down we had all better be in the same boat. Oxford was not likely to be the subject of enemy bombing, being of no importance militarily, industrially—or, the High Table wags added, academically.

Russian Visits

Jean's gift of tongues amazes me: she speaks French and German, has a smattering of Swedish and Italian, and knows enough Russian to make civil remarks when the occasion calls for it. This last accomplishment came into use on a brief visit to Moscow, where I had been invited to lecture in the Institutes of the Academy of Science. As a treat, we were also taken on a trip to Leningrad. We arrived at Moscow airport on the morning of our departure to find that the plane from Leningrad to Moscow, whose turn-around was to be our plane from Moscow to Leningrad, had been delayed by a severe snowstorm. Our Intourist interpreter was somewhat put out by this, probably thinking (quite mistakenly) that we were saying to each other 'Oh it's those bloody inefficient Russians again.' After a couple of hours we were told that a plane was waiting for us and we travelled to Leningrad almost alone in a DC-3 which had been made available to us by the simple expedient of standing off all the passengers to its intended destination—Minsk, I think—and putting the plane at our disposal. Jean and I were horrified and we told the interpreter that if such a thing were to occur in Great Britain, even, say, for the Prime Minister, there would be such a flaming row that the government would probably fall. Our interpreter was not impressed, probably because he had no conception of what was meant by the notion of a government's falling. To Jean and me the entire incident was an eye-opener and we wondered how such an action would be excused and condoned by our fellow-traveller friends back at home.

In Leningrad we were dazzled, as everyone is, by the Rembrandts and the Dutch paintings in the Hermitage and we were finally introduced to a vain and elderly pedant called General Pavlovsky who would not let us leave the premises without taking two or three plaster heads of himself, one of which was a gift for an English friend while the others were to be treasured by ourselves. At the opera we saw a Rimsky-Korsakov spectacular which included a realistic on-stage fire. The music was not very gripping—a judgement that will not surprise musically minded people who all hate Rimsky's guts for having rewritten Mussorgsky in the course of producing an 'on ice' version of *Boris Godunov*—but the spectacle, I must say, was at least equal to the old-fashioned Drury Lane spectaculars I can remember my mother having taken me to see. One such, *Good Luck*, included a ship's putting out to sea, a frighteningly realistic conflagration, and—the dramatic highpoint—a horse-race on the stage in which to everybody's disappointment the horse that won was the one intended to do so.

This was not my only visit to Russia. On the initiative of the British Council I paid a second visit in 1966 in company with James Gowans, then the head of an MRC unit, and Professor Roy Calne, the foremost English transplant surgeon. We were to familiarize ourselves with the character and quality of the research on transplantation in progress in the Soviet Union. It was not a joyous visit, partly because we got a bit fed up with hearing each other's lectures so often and partly because Russian research, generally speaking, was inferior to a degree which we should not have credited if we had been told beforehand it was so. When we visited an Institute and enquired civilly about the work in progress the Director merely recited the programme of research approved either by the University, the Academy of Sciences, or a Ministry or some other authority, presumably on the grounds that they could certainly not be doing anything more or less than they were officially authorized to do. After listening to one such recital by the director of the research programme, Roy Calne, hidden by large dark glasses, asked impatiently 'But what were your results?' Gowans and I felt, as our hosts did, that Roy had committed a solecism, and we did our best to divert the conversation.

The most disgraceful single episode happened in Lumumba University when we visited a pathologist who showed us a lump of plastic containing a length of long bone. Such a dried piece, he told us, was suitable for grafting to repair gaps in living bone; this was not surprising, but we were amazed when he told us that the cells in the preserved bone were still alive and had been shown to be so by tissue-culture tests. This is impossible, and the speaker probably knew it and could see that we didn't believe a word he said. By the time we left Lumumba University Jim Gowans was beginning to feel his time was being wasted, even squandered, and muttered what a pity it was that we had heard nothing but 'Lmumbo jumbo'. Most unhappily his father had become ill during our visit to Russia and arrangements were courteously and quickly made to transport him home, much to my envy, because I had simulated what I had believed to be a very serious cough, accompanied by what Jane Austen would have called 'a putrid fever', and had asked my hosts to arrange for my own speedy return. But Russia was—and probably is still —a place where people keep on getting ill in an old-fashioned sort of way, so my simulated illness caused no stir.

At one point I asked our interpreter if poliomyelitis was a problem in Russia. Now the interpreter had come to hear that poliomyelitis was, epidemiologically speaking, an affliction of well-to-do countries like America and Sweden, and was put out by my imputation that Russia might not suffer from an upper-class disease. So—yes, he proudly assured us, poliomyelitis was indeed rife in Russia.

Collaboration

Many of Jean's and my friends who know very well that Jean has been my life-support system since my first illness do not know how much she has relieved me, all our married life, of duties and chores that might hinder the prosecution of scientific research—for example, I have owned several leaseholds or freeholds during the course of my life but I have never known anything about them. Jean has looked after them, and almost everything else of a tiresome or distracting nature.

My first stroke was not the only one Jean helped me

through. By 1980 I had recovered well enough to walk about a mile—with a stick and not very elegantly. In March we flew to New York and I managed to get from 65th Street to Sam Goody's store on W. 49th Street, where I stood for an hour choosing wonderful records of Edwardian opera singers. My role in New York was to deliver a Commencement Address at the Sloan Kettering Cancer Center. The delivery of commencement addresses is not a favoured art form of mine and my antipathy to it was given added weight by finding that when I reached the rostrum the speaking notes which I had put there in readiness for my performance had been picked up by mistake and taken away by the previous speaker. Luckily, I know by heart long passages of the writing of Sir Francis Bacon, and my good memory and power to improvise pulled me through;· but at the reception held afterwards I had a very severe turn of nausea and vertigo of the kind which very often, I understand, is the outward evidence of a brain-stem lesion. In this case the trouble turned out to be a blockage of a brain-stem vessel by a blood-platelet thrombus. I was accordingly taken to Memorial Hospital, where I received the superb professional attention of Dr Jerome Posner and his staff. I was well looked after by the nursing staff, observing with satisfaction that many of the most popular nurses were those who had been trained in the British Isles. Nurses in American hospitals, it should be explained, are much more specialized than English nurses. Each major ward has its 'intravenous team' of deft specialists who take blood for clinical tests, and set up intravenous drips.

As in English hospitals, the menu for meals was à la carte and one's entries on the checklist were scanned and priced by a computer, a circumstance that led one rather naïve nurse to tell me that food in the hospital was provided by computer.

Through a dispensation made possible by our friend Lewis Thomas's being Chancellor of the whole huge complex of Hospital and Cancer Research Centre, Jean was enabled to sleep in my room and helped to nurse me, kind friends making sure she did not dine alone. Dr Posner said my presence was good for the department's morale because my affliction was very much less grievous than those suffered by the majority of the patients who either had brain tumours or were recovering from operations for their removal. I improved daily, but I have not got back to the condition in which it was possible for me to do that walk from Sam Goody's to midtown New York. In my room in Memorial Hospital I had what I think is described as a 'cardiac' bed, one in which the patient has a console which he can operate to raise his head, feet, or knees. We arranged to go home as soon as I was fit to travel, and Jean and I wondered if such a bed would be available in the wards of Northwick Park Hospital. 'I expect there will be one,' I said, 'and it will probably be operated by steam.' But when I did come home I was received with the utmost kindness and had quite a de luxe electric bed. As my ward was quite near my office in the Clinical Research Centre I was able to carry on with my work and later on to dress and go daily to my office. All my friends rallied round and Jean was again beside me. My second stint in hospital was far from disagreeable. I had plenty to think about, because I had undertaken to deliver a lecture at a joint meeting of the Royal Society of London and its American opposite number, the American Philosophical Society of Philadelphia. I had written most of it in my head lying in bed in Memorial Hospital and all that now remained was to dictate it.* I could not deliver it myself because I was having difficulty in co-ordinating speech with breathing, an affliction for which the hospital administered professional speech therapy; but I did not think I could rely upon my voice to do justice to my contribution to the joint meeting, so I asked the Big Chief, Sir James Gowans, if he would deliver it for me and happily he agreed to do so—and agreed also with what I had to say.

Unhappily a year or two later my blood platelets created a new opportunity for God to move in that mysterious way which endears Him to the devout: I suffered thrombosis of the retinal vessels of my left eye, which later had to be

---

* This lecture, 'Can Scientific Discovery be Premeditated?' is published in my *The Limits of Science* (New York 1984; Oxford, 1985), 45–54.

removed and replaced by a plastic eye, not quite a perfect match in colour for the other, because the 'beer-bottle brown with a merry twinkle' I had specified could not easily be matched.

My illnesses have had one unexpectedly happy consequence. When I am asked nowadays to attend a conference or give a course of lectures I write back to say that the Committee that proposed my name for the distinction will need to reconsider their choice when I tell them that I cannot get on without the companionship of my wife—which would double the travelling and subsistence expenses that my acceptance would necessarily entail. No invitation has ever been withdrawn, however, and Jean always accompanies me on my many travels abroad, though she often sings for her supper too, by lecturing on her own special human–ecological, conservation, and population control interests. I have continued writing books—a habit-forming activity, as all authors come to know. Now Jean and I have taken to writing books together, and it has proved a happy collaboration because Jean likes and has a very good ear for my style: when she goes over the pieces I draft they end up more like my writing than they were to begin with.

The two books we have so far written together are *The Life Science* (in 1977) and a book of aphorisms or short essays, *Aristotle to Zoos: A Philosophic Dictionary of Biology*. We expressed a low opinion of the claim made on Aristotle's behalf that he was a scientist and moreover one of great distinction—a view which aroused a lot of indignation, principally, I suspect, from people who, just as Aristotle would have done, did not actually read our criticisms but felt that we must be mistaken.

Of my own writings, the most successful in the judgement of the market-place was *Advice to a Young Scientist* (1979). This aroused some resentment among those who had attempted and failed the intelligence test it embodied. At the risk of arousing further resentment, I reproduce it here:

To many eyes, many of the figures (particularly the holy ones) of El Greco's paintings seem unnaturally tall and thin. An ophthalmologist who shall be nameless surmised that they were drawn so because El Greco suffered a defect of vision that made him *see* people that way, and as he saw them, so he would necessarily draw them.

Can such an interpretation be valid? When putting this question, sometimes to large academic audiences, I have added, 'Anyone who can see *instantly* that this explanation is nonsense and is nonsense for philosophic rather than aesthetic reasons is undoubtedly bright. On the other hand, anyone who still can't see it is nonsense even when its nonsensicality is explained must be rather dull.' The explanation is epistemological—that is, it has to do with the theory of knowledge.

Suppose a painter's defect of vision was, as it might easily have been, diplopia—in effect, of seeing everything double. If the ophthalmologist's explanation were right, then such a painter would paint his figures double—twenty-four at the Last Supper then, *two* stags at bay and so on; but if he did so, then when he came to inspect his handiwork, would he not see all the figures fourfold and maybe suspect that something was amiss? If a defect of vision is in question, the only figures that could seem natural (that is, representational) to the painter must seem natural to us also, even if we ourselves suffer defects of vision; if some of El Greco's figures seem unnaturally tall and thin, they appear so because this was El Greco's intention.

Advice to a Young Scientist was an extended write-up of a topic on which I had often lectured, and the same goes for my most recent book *The Limits of Science*, the purpose of which was to explain why science, though seemingly all-powerful, was quite unable (in principle) to answer those ultimate questions which have to do with the nature, purpose, and destiny of mankind. I believe these answers are to be found, if at all, in religion, metaphysics, or imaginative literature. My adoption of a non-religious attitude throughout represents my own non-religious (I do not say *anti*-religious) feelings, for religion has not sustained me on any of the occasions when the comfort it professes to give would have been most welcome.

The relationship between care and solicitude and virtually complete dependence does not necessarily lead to a loving relationship, but Jean and I are so constituted that with us it has done so and the present period of our life is a very happy one. There is one disquieting thought, though, that takes some of the warmth out of the winter sunshine: the Way of the World under its present management, which leaves very much to be desired, is such that one or other of us must one day go it alone. This is something we think of no more often than merely prudential considerations require, because the best remedy for disquieting thoughts is to abstain from thinking them.

ON LIVING A BIT LONGER

I am one of those who believes that a good life—one that is worth living—might well last a bit longer than it normally does. I attach a table compiled mainly from Swedish data showing the mean expectation of life of men and women at various ages over a 200-year period. Some of the variables that affect life expectancy are approaching limiting values—among them mortality at or around birth. Clearly there is room for improvement about expectancy towards life's end. However, most discussion of the matter has been obfuscated by the condemnation of such an ambition as impious and socially destructive, as if that could settle the matter once and for all.

TABLE

Mean Expectation of Life of Males and Females
in Sweden over Two Centuries

Period		Mean Expectation at Age		
		0	60	80
1755–76	Male	33.20	12.24	4.27
	Female	35.70	13.08	4.47
1856–60	Male	40.48	13.12	3.12
	Female	44.15	14.04	4.91
1936–40	Male	64.30	16.35	5.25
	Female	66.90	17.19	5.49
1971–5	Male	72.07	17.65	6.08
	Female	77.65	21.29	7.28

We can witness already the first stirrings of research of which the end result may be the prolongation of active life by the consumption of antoxidant substances. I cannot summarize the matter more briefly than in the essay I wrote for the 'Futures' section of the *Guardian* under the heading 'Four Score Years and Ten—and Still Counting' (13 December 1984). What follows is a slightly edited version of that essay.

Four Score Years and Ten—and Still Counting

It is the great glory and also the great threat of science that anything which is possible in principle—which does not flout a bedrock law of physics—can be done if the intention to do it is sufficiently resolute and long sustained. If therefore a scientific enterprise threatens to endanger or radically to alter our style of life it should be subjected to political scrutiny before being embarked upon—I mean a scrutiny from outside science that gives more weight to moral, social, and prudential considerations than scientists ordinarily give them. Consider in this light the prevalence of the notion that our span of active life might well be extended. Over the past few years the advocacy of Linus Pauling and the experiments of Denham Harman of the University of Nebraska have shown that the lives of laboratory animals can be extended 20–25 per cent by the administration of fairly high doses of substances related to industrial antoxidants. There is no doubt about the authenticity of the experiments: one such was done under my nose by Alex Comfort and his colleagues I. Youhotsky-Gore and K. Pathmanathan in the Zoology Department of University College London. The interpretation of these findings is ambiguous. The mice thus fed will indeed live longer—but is this, as Denham Harman thinks, because antoxidants annul the otherwise destructive action of free radicles on very small biological structures, or could it be because antoxidants are so disagreeable that they seriously put mice off their wittles—thus in effect reproducing the classic experiments by McCay and his colleagues which showed that calorie starvation effectively prolongs life? If these findings in mice and rats could be reproduced in human beings, their effect would be that a man of ninety would have the same energy and address as a seventy-year-old—and so proportionately at other ages; then people would begin to think of our allotted life as *four* score years and ten.

Some professional or amateur gerontologists are keen to try to reproduce their laboratory findings in human beings. Now is this an irreverent and foolhardy escapade which will surely have evil consequences or a bold and exciting scientific adventure of the kind Sir Francis Bacon would have applauded? Consider first the charge of irreverence: it was not God who said that our lifespan was three score years and ten, it was a poet (Psalm 90: 10). Poets are sometimes more influenced by rhyme and metre than by empirical truth or even sense. So it was, for example, with John Dryden in the lines that helped to perpetuate the gothic illusion of a close connection between genius and insanity:

> Great wits are sure to madness near alli'd,
> And thin partitions do their bounds divide.

Even the psalmist did not say he was *sure*.

People temperamentally opposed to attempts to prolong life are fond of quoting Walter Savage Landor's

> Nature I loved, and next to Nature, Art;
> I warmed both hands before the fire of life;
> It sinks, and I am ready to depart.

In Aldous Huxley's *Crome Yellow* a young man taking leave of his hosts taps the barometer in the entrance hall, sees it fall and says—hoping to be overheard and counted as a wit—'It sinks and I am ready to depart.' This is the best comment known to me on Landor's spiritless affirmation.

Healthy and cared-for people have reasons enough to live a few more years—to see how the grandchildren turn out and if the unfolding of history corroborates or confutes their expectations of the way things will go; and a gardener who may have just been replanting a south-facing bed will surely want to gratify the joyous expectation of another spring.

Is the attempt to prolong human life a premeditated insult to nature—an attempt to substitute the inmates of a geriatric ward with the bounding, exuberant, yea-saying folk we were when the world was young? People weren't, of course. Much nearer the truth was Thomas Hobbes's belief that before the coming of Leviathan, that great organism of State, the life of man was solitary, poor, nasty, brutish, and short—and as a rule, ailing too. The 'good old days' argument cuts no ice in medical circles. The time will come when we look back upon the ideology of three score years and ten much as we look back now on the days when a woman would have to bear seven to ten children in the hope of bringing four or five to adult life.

The prolongation of a good life, happy and healthy, is fully in keeping with the spirit of medicine and is in a sense the very consummation of all that medical research has worked towards, *for all advances in medicine increase life-expectancy*. Even a couple of aspirin tablets taken daily might circumvent a platelet crisis and so be seen on an epidemiological scale to increase life-expectancy. The same would go for putting a plaster on a cut finger, something that will infinitesimally reduce the chances of septicaemia, and so on. The prolongation of life will increase population size at a time when there are enough people in the world already, and although the people added will be post-reproductive in age they will still eat and occupy space and consume energy. A graver problem is the burden upon a caring State of pensions and medical care, a burden falling disproportionately on the young. Moreover, working years and provisions for pensions will have to change. These are grave problems but they are not insoluble, for social changes of an essentially similar kind have happened over the past two hundred years, during which the mean expectation of life rose from about 30 to between 60 and 70, and anyhow the changes are not going to take place overnight. Consider the changes since Jane Austen's day. In her first novel *Sense and Sensibility* the elderly Colonel Brandon seeks the hand of a romantic young girl, Marianne Dashwood. In Marianne's view he is an old man who should be thinking not of matrimony but of woolly underwear and how best to avoid draughts. How old then was this amorous old dotard? He was just over thirty-five, we read; and when the question arises of purchasing an annuity for Marianne's mother, a 'healthy woman of forty', it is thought most unlikely that she will live until the age of fifty-five. Suppose now that some prescient man were to have told Jane Austen's characters that over the next century the mean expectation of life at all ages would double—something much more far reaching than the modest 20–25 per cent we now have here in mind—would not Jane Austen's characters have been very mistaken to have been shocked by the riskiness and impiety of such a possibility? The great social adaptation was, however, made and there is no reason to think it cannot be made again. Let us take care that people as far distant from us as we are from the world of Jane Austen do not have reason to pity us for being so faint spirited. But there is an element of risk: we cannot foresee all the distant consequences of increasing life-expectancy, especially in respect of the risk of cancer and perhaps of Alzheimer's disease, senile dementia, and many may think this element of uncertainty should turn us away from our project. What I believe will happen is that some enthusiasts, especially in California, will go ahead with the longevity project to purchase extra years of life at the risk of contracting senile dementia and for its own reward. Francis Bacon, though pious and deeply religious, was the first advocate of just this kind of adventurousness in science, and would have approved: 'The true aim of Science', he wrote in his little-known *Valerius Terminus*, 'is the discovery of all operations and all possibilities of operations from immortality (if it were possible) to the meanest mechanical practice.'

Bacon, then, was on my side. We already have a moral commitment to biomedical research which increases life-expectancy and I see no reason to think that the highway of medical melioration that has brought us so far already will now lead us into evil. We have long since been travelling that road and it is too late now to cease to be ambitious.

This is all very fine, but we have no scientific authority either to believe or to doubt that the results of these laboratory experiments on the longevity of animals are applicable to man. Inspired by these findings our own practice is to take 5g of ascorbic acid (vitamin C) every day, and 2,000 IU of vitamin E—an antoxidant widely used in manufactures to prevent the rancidification of fats, especially vegetable oils. Gestures such as these will be thought timid by American colleagues who take 10g a day and excessive by people naïve enough to suppose that the metabolic function of vitamin C in nature is to prevent scurvy. It may be that we have by luck hit upon a good compromise, but whether we have or not I have no intention of preparing any last words, partly because I do not expect to be in a garrulous mood and partly because the utterance of last words is a deeply unsatisfactory art form. I am certain though that my last *thoughts* will be of Jean and that, so far as they concern my life generally, I shall be thinking that in spite of its vicissitudes my life has by no means been without its risible aspects.

INDEX